BLACK MANIFESTO

BLACK
MANIFESTO

Religion, Racism, and Reparations

Edited by ROBERT S. LECKY
and H. ELLIOTT WRIGHT

A SEARCH BOOK
SHEED AND WARD · NEW YORK

For
Viola Cox
who lives in Nashville

Acknowledgment

IN ADDITION to the contributors who wrote for this volume on relatively short deadlines, many others directly and indirectly assisted the editors. Special appreciation is expressed to Lillian R. Block, managing editor of Religious News Service, for permitting the files of the agency to be consulted. The thorough and objective RNS treatment of the Manifesto phenomenon was particularly valuable in preparing the chronology, found in the Appendix, of the initial months.

Thanks is also due to Charles Lerrigo, most likely the nation's most informed journalist on the National Black Economic Development Conference and the issues it has raised for the religious community. Mr. Lerrigo offered worthy suggestions and read the introduction and chronology for factual accuracy. A similar task was performed by Kay Longcope of the Interreligious Foundation for Community Organization (IFCO). She merits grateful appreciation.

The Rev. Lucius Walker, director of IFCO; Dr. Ernest Campbell, preaching minister of the Riverside Church; Arthur Moore, editor of World Outlook and Religious News Service: each graciously gave permission to reprint documents found in the Appendix.

Others who must receive public acknowledgment for helpfulness are Betty Thompson and the Rev. Grant Shockley, both of the United Methodist Board of Missions; L. I. Stell, Jr., of the Department of Information of the National Council of

Churches; Tyler Breeze, a student at Union Theological Seminary, New York; Emily Dieter of the Riverside Church; Walter Boyd of the Office of Communication of the Episcopal Church; Marjorie Hyer, a free lance journalist; Joseph McLellan and Gerrard Hekker of RNS, and Leon Howell and Juanita Wright, both formerly of *Christianity and Crisis* magazine.

In particular and special ways Doreen Graves, of the National Council's Department of Social Justice, and Rev. James McGraw, an editor of *Renewal* magazine, contributed to the realization of this volume.

Finally, but importantly, thanks is given to Philip Scharper and Leonard Mayhew of Sheed and Ward for encouragement and for agreeing to a stepped-up production schedule.

Robert S. Lecky and H. Elliott Wright
New York City
Independence Day, 1969

Contributors and Editors

ROBERT BROWNE teaches economics at Fairleigh Dickinson University, Teaneck, N.J. Much in demand as a speaker, he gave the keynote address at the National Black Economic Development Conference in Detroit, April 25, 1969. Dr. Browne is BEDC Eastern vice-chairman.

HARVEY G. COX, professor in the Harvard University Divinity School, stands at the fountainhead of the modern stress on church responsibility within the secular world. He is author of the best-selling *The Secular City*, other books and many articles.

JAMES FORMAN is director of international affairs for the Student Non-Violent Coordinating Committee and head of BEDC's United Black Appeal. The major spokesman for the Black Manifesto, he lives in New York.

DICK GREGORY has successfully mixed a career as comedian with his role as a militant black spokesman. A candidate for the presidency in 1968, he is the author of a number of books, including *Nigger: An Autobiography* and *Shadow that Scares Me*.

JAMES M. LAWSON, pastor of Centenary United Methodist Church, Memphis, is the most articulate living advocate of nonviolent social change. Chairman of Black Methodists for Church Renewal, he was an organizer of Southern sit-ins during the early 1960's.

ROBERT S. LECKY, a native of Australia and a Methodist clergyman, is former associate editor of *Christianity and Crisis* magazine and now associated with the experimental department of the National Council of Churches. He is coauthor of *Can These Bones Live?: The Failure of Church Renewal.*

STEPHEN C. ROSE is a noted young commentator on the modern church. Former editor of *Renewal* magazine, he is editor-at-large of *Christianity and Crisis* and author of *The Grass Roots Church* and *Alarms and Visions: Churches and the American Crisis.* He lives in Massachusetts.

WILLIAM STRINGFELLOW, an attorney, is an eminent theologian. Once associated with the East Harlem Protestant Parish, he is author of many books, including *My People Is the Enemy, A Private and Public Faith* and *Dissenter in a Great Society.* He lives in Rhode Island.

H. ELLIOTT WRIGHT is coauthor with Mr. Lecky of *Can These Bones Live?* Protestant editor of Religious News Service, he writes for a wide range of publications and is a former staff member of *motive* magazine. A native of Alabama, Mr. Wright lives in New York City.

Contents

APPENDICES

REPARATIONS NOW?
AN INTRODUCTION

by ROBERT S. LECKY
and H. ELLIOTT WRIGHT

SHOULD WHITE PEOPLE, the majority in the United States, pay reparations to black people for two centuries of forced slavery and another hundred years of black servitude to white structures? The question is one of the most perplexing, challenging and emotion-producing of the times. And it is one of the most current and unavoidable.

This book is an investigation of the issue, with particular reference to the time and the way in which demands for reparations for blacks became a public force. It focuses on the predominantly white religious institutions to which the demands were first made. A proposal that reparations be paid to 24–30 million blacks raises hosts of thorny questions for both whites and blacks: Who pays? Who gets (after all, some blacks are affluent)? Who administers? What programs and channels would be most helpful? What responsibility would well-off whites have for still worse-off blacks after a set sum was paid? What would be the implications for future race relations?

All these questions have been talked about, written about and shouted about since May, 1969, and there is no reason to believe their importance has passed or will soon fade. This volume attempts to bring together comment on the reparations controversy along with documentation and data on its launching which have not before been widely available to concerned and wondering citizens of all races.

Editorial intentions here are neither polemic nor apologetic. Rather, the purpose is to offer a forum for religious discussion, since it was to the churches and synagogues that reparation demands initially came. When strategies for improving the economic plight of long-persecuted minorities are pushed to logical conclusions, the discussion extends beyond religious boundaries. The contents of this book can hopefully point directions for the reparations discussion as it expands into other areas.

Since no essay which follows gives a chronicle of events surrounding the appearance of the Black Manifesto announcing reparation demands, the Introduction is meant to put the issue in an historical setting. Concentration is on developments and representative reactions through the first three months of the Manifesto's existence. The date is not arbitrarily chosen. It was dictated by events. By the end of July, 1969, most major religious groups in the nation had received Manifesto demands or had responded before receiving them. A majority of the black leaders were on record about the reparations question. Finally, a federal investigation centering on the Manifesto and its supporters was in progress. Such a turn was the first major step moving outside the religious context and therefore beyond the sphere of the Manifesto's original religious environment, which is the topic of this study. The investigation itself was a sign that evaluation of, or results produced by, the Manifesto will never be totally divorced from the volatile period of its infancy.

Someday a detailed, scholarly history of the Black Manifesto and its ramifications can be written, but only in a day when its programs have been implemented, or when the document itself has been washed from emotions. That time is not yet.

Reflections on matters such as religion's financial ability to pay reparations are also in order in this Introduction, as are references to documents found in the Appendix. A reading of the Manifesto, reprinted in the Appendix, may be a helpful first step. Following the text is a Chronology relevant to the Manifesto's public impact in its early months.

Religion, Racism and Reparations

The news media across America recorded "shock" when on May 4, James Forman, a black militant leader, interrupted Sunday morning worship at New York's famed interdenominational, interracial Riverside Church. He presented Black Manifesto demands for that congregation's "share" of $500 million from the U.S. white religious community.

As the Manifesto phenomenon spread, shock mingled with outrage, deep concern and confusion during the following weeks. Many religious groups received Forman visitations, though he himself did not continue the practice of personally interrupting worship. Riverside had an injunction against worship disruption issued. Denominational offices and church facilities in many cities were temporarily taken over to underscore specific demands, which on June 13 Mr. Forman said should be collectively raised to three billion dollars. Local black groups picked up the cause and the tactics. Injunctions came and went. New York's Interchurch Center had a restraining order for some weeks. Mr. Forman promised no further disruption to agencies there while consultations with the National Council of Churches proceeded in the late summer. Pro and con polarizations of various compositions were forthcoming.

Before Summer 1969 officially arrived, less than two months after the Manifesto was promulgated by a National Black Economic Development Conference (NBEDC), Mr. Forman, the Manifesto and reparations had substantially changed the face of the race struggle. Manifesto-centered events caused greater vibrations in the U.S. religious world than any other single human rights development in a decade of monumental happenings.

(At a meeting of the steering committee of the conference in mid-July, the word "National" was dropped from the name of the organization sponsoring the Manifesto. In this Introduction, the initials BEDC are used to designate the organization, while NBEDC is used to mean the meeting where the Manifesto originated.)

Some whites wanted to disregard the whole matter at first,

treating Mr. Forman as an individual with little following in the black community. Among black churchmen and civil rights workers, opposition and skepticism were not infrequent. Doctor J. H. Jackson, president of the 6.5 million member National Baptist Convention, U.S.A., Inc.,—the third largest Protestant denomination in the country—scored Manifesto programs and methods. He compared the document to the Communist Manifesto of 1848. Doctor Jackson had never identified himself closely with the black power movement. The well-known *Amsterdam News* of Harlem was editorially unsympathetic to Forman strategies. Black clergy groups were far from unanimous in endorsing Manifesto tactics.

But Mr. Forman was not alone. Black militants outside the church, members and clergy of all-black denominations and blacks in mostly white churches backed the BEDC. Some blacks who were formerly cautious in asserting the cause of racial justice found stronger voices. The Spanish-American minority began to utilize the reparation ideology. Even had Mr. Forman been a lone figure, the repercussions within the white churches were too intensive to be ignored. A new chapter in the drive for human equality was opened.

What was new? Disturbances in houses of worship were rare, but hardly novel. Church walk-outs, walk-ins and even scuffles had occurred before in the 1960's. Black militancy and demands directed to white institutions were not introduced in Riverside's sanctuary. Several ingredients were new. One was a Manifesto rhetoric more militant, threatening and revolutionary than most churchmen were accustomed to hearing. Another was the large financial claims on what to some was already the most liberal, though poorest, segment of society, religion. Many white religious leaders were shocked to be told their goodwill was neither good nor wilful enough.

Still a third new factor was the linking of economic reparations to religion in the fight against racism and poverty. An implication was that organized religion might have more influence than it thought it had. The rapid, emotional course of events after the first Sunday in May somewhat shoved aside the more serious considerations of how and why the Black Manifesto linked religion, racism and reparations. Did connection more solid than an alliteration of words predating the Manifesto exist? At least, churches and synagogues were forced to consider the possibility by the BEDC initiatives.

Reparation is no new idea in America, but demands for financial restitution from religion were unprecedented before the Black Manifesto. Eugene Carson Blake, the American who is chief executive of the World Council of Churches, was likely right when he said the Manifesto came to the church because of what Christians and Jews have confessed about human dignity. In terms of religion's claim to be equipped to explore the moral dimensions of economics, culture and politics, perhaps the target of the Manifesto had providential direction. Scores of white churchmen were willing to concede that likelihood. Few held out dollars to the BEDC, yet from expected and unexpected quarters came thanksgiving to God that Mr. Forman and the Manifesto had given religion an opportunity to be socially relevant. It was, undoubtedly, also a frightening realization. Somebody *was* listening, or seeming to listen, to modern, mainstream religion's verbal positions on justice, human welfare and a better global future.

Religion and Civil Rights: Background

In the mid-1950's churches and synagogues hesitantly involved themselves in the civil rights movement springing up after the U.S. Supreme Court outlawed public school segregation. Momentum built up, and by the early 1960's religious groups were in what appeared as the vanguard traveling the legislative and nonviolent path toward implementing the provisions of the federal constitution and the Jewish-Christian confession about brotherly love. Segregation was the foe.

Public inertia frustrated the promises of the hard-won civil rights laws. Public apathy to the needs of the traditionally oppressed turned legal equality into ghoulish hypocrisy for many black Americans. Some religious leaders were sympathetic to the black power cries heard at mid-decade, to the impatience reflected in ghetto turbulence, and to black community organizations willing to postpone integration for the sake of black self-determination. Laws alone were proved in-

sufficient to solve the problems growing out of three centuries
of white racism. Watts in 1966 and Newark and Detroit in
1967 were clear indication that the struggle must continue.

A black economic foundation to give substance to black
equality in a material-oriented, capitalist society increasingly
became the civil rights goal in the late sixties. Before his
murder in 1968, Dr. Martin Luther King, Jr., had turned
the efforts of the Southern Christian Leadership Conference
to economic development, with the King-planned Poor People's
Campaign of Summer 1968, aimed at winning an economic
program from the federal government.

The general situation, coupled with Dr. King's assassination in April and the report of the National Advisory Commission on Civil Disorders (Kerner Commission) in March,
produced a swell of religious attention to minority group
development. The Kerner report put the major blame for urban
riots on white racism and warned that the U.S. was moving
toward two separate, unequal, white and black groupings.

Local, regional and national Christian and Jewish agencies
vowed to fight racism and poverty. They also took some responsibility for the continuing discrimination. The conserva-
tively religious were even mobilized to voice corrective intentions. Interreligious coalitions for social efforts multiplied. By
Fall 1968 nearly $50 million had been pledged and some
millions expended.

It is doubtful that the Black Manifesto could have come
forth had the religious groups not adopted such strong antipoverty rhetoric. Charles Spivey, Jr., director of Social Justice
for the National Council of Churches, suggested this when
he said the Manifesto told churches to "put up or shut up."

The pledges were not insincere, but they probably did
ignore signs saying well-motivated intentions were not adequate to handle the enormity of the problems. As early as
1966, the former National Committee of Negro Churchmen
expressed dissatisfaction with the white religious sphere's
tendency to reflect the broader white culture by taking paternalistic approaches—white directed—to the obliteration of
poverty and discrimination. Despite the financial commitments
of mid-1968, greater displeasure was evident when the by then

National Committee of Black Churchmen met in late October. Reactions to paternalism were loud. The applause was rousing when a speaker declared: "Let the church see that the Black Power Movement is assuming power and consolidating power, then the white church seeks to coopt it by funding its community organization programs and then coopting its leaders. The whites are always in control. They dictate what must be done."

The year 1968 saw a boom of denominational, diocesan and religious agency concern about the "crisis in the nation"— racism, violence and poverty. Antedating this boom by almost a year was the Interreligious Foundation for Community Organization (IFCO). It began in September 1967 as a cooperative venture to fund locally-based organizations upgrading the conditions of the poor and offering participation and self-determination to people shut out of power. IFCO was not a black organization in terms of directors, nor was it completely slanted toward black poverty. However, the plight of blacks could hardly fail to be a major focus in light of socio-economic realities.

Then IFCO members grew to twenty-five between October 1967 and June 1969, with each paying $1,000 to join. Major religious agencies signing up were the American Baptist Home Mission Societies, the National Division of the United Methodist Board of Missions, the Board of Christian Social Concerns of that denomination, the Executive Council of the Episcopal Church, the Boards of National Ministries and Christian Education of the Presbyterian Church, U.S., the United Presbyterian Board of National Missions, the Board for Homeland Ministries of the United Church of Christ, the Board of American Missions of the Luthern Church in America, the American Jewish Committee and the National Catholic Conference for Interracial Justice.

The going was not easy. Administrative snags were many. One question was the degree of IFCO control over the projects funded. Many members, including some of the larger church boards, gave nothing more than the initial fee. As of May 1969, only 3.6 percent of the nearly $1.5 million allocated in project training and special grants had come from Jewish

and Catholic participants, according to the Reverend Lucius
Walker, IFCO director and a black American Baptist clergyman.

During the first year the Episcopal Church gave a $200,000
matching grant but then instituted expenditure restrictions on
further contributions. United Presbyterians offered $20,000 in
undesignated funds and $127,000 for special projects. Most
significant in terms of size was $200,000 from the 1.5 million
member American Baptist Convention, one of the smaller
IFCO denominations. The foundation's early experience was
not dissimilar from that of the "Crisis in the Nation" program
of the National Council of Churches. It found that instead of
giving money to consolidated ecumenical or interreligious
minority economic development, the churches set up individual, often competitive, emergency efforts.

NBEDC and the Manifesto

It was IFCO, a year after it was launched, which laid plans
for a National Black Economic Development Conference. Held
in Detroit from April 25–27 in a Wayne State University
building, the meeting was not structured to produce the
NBEDC as a continuing organization (which it became with
existence independent of IFCO) or to end up with a Black
Manifesto. It was, rather, to bring together a broad spectrum
of black leaders to explore strategies for more rapid black-
directed community development. It was to be like a Quaker
meeting where issues are "threshed out." Workshops were
arranged; speakers invited.

The need for such a gathering, as well as the results, must
be seen in relation to social realities becoming clear in the
months between September 1967 and April 1969. Among these
was decreasing hope in the promise given by the government's
war on poverty. The relative failure of the poverty program
to provide adequate correctives to unemployment, health, educational needs and poor housing was widely recognized before
the presidential election year 1968. The government had stood
as the source of legal impetus and funds for social improvement in civil rights and religious thrusts. Would it make ap-

propriation commensurate with the needs? Could it do so and continue the Vietnam War?

Attitudes of the new Nixon Administration toward social issues were, at best, ambiguous as 1969 approached. The government's future plans for poverty alleviation and its degree of sensitivity toward minority ambitions were unknown. The rejection of Mr. Nixon as a candidate by most black leaders suggested lean expectations for aggressive federal incentives. Moreover, the new President's "black capitalism" proposals struck militant and ghetto-based blacks as far too modest to be capitalistic or greatly beneficial for the masses of blacks.

Government intransigency before pressure from the poor had already been demonstrated at Resurrection City, the encampment pitched in Washington, D.C., as the first phase of the Poor People's Campaign. And this had the psychological weight of Dr. King's murder behind it! The Poor People's Campaign was met with more criticism for causing a tourist eyesore in the shadow of the Lincoln Memorial than with concern for the poor. Limited church support was about the only institutional backing the campaign received.

In early 1968 nobody had rushed to implement the recommendations of the Kerner Commission. Hands were wrung over the escalating racial polarization described by the blue ribbon panel. Talk was plentiful but, as the adage goes, it was cheap.

As 1969 progressed, the notable, verbally lauded black-proposed economic development recommendations had not become national priorities nor been scheduled for congressional hearings. The "Domestic Marshall Plan" of the National Urban League lay dormant. The "Freedom Budget" of the A. Philip Randolph Institute was a paper document three years after it was announced by the venerated Mr. Randolph, president emeritus of the Brotherhood of Sleeping Car Porters. When the labor leader marked his eightieth birthday in early 1969, tributes lacked a commitment to put into effect his request that $185 billion be spent over a ten year period to free millions of Americans from poverty and deprivation.

This is not to say that black conditions were as bad in 1969 as they had been a decade earlier. They were not. Barriers of all kinds had fallen. Black college graduates were finding better jobs. Black public officials were increasing. Discrimination was outlawed. But for a majority of the millions of blacks first-class citizenship was in the future. Hard-core black unemployment persisted. Ghettos were still mostly slums. More importantly, blacks did not feel the white power structures either listened to them or allowed them the freedom of shaping their future. To militants, even the "Freedom Budget" and the "Domestic Marshall Plan" would be too contingent on saying "please" to whites. Black begging was going out of style.

From an atmosphere cluttered with paper promises the participants came to the Detroit conference called by IFCO. It was a black, black meeting. White pledges, white power and white plans for blacks were left outside. The conference received a "bad press," no doubt partly because white journalists were also excluded. Except in black papers, the Black Manifesto itself was hardly reported when it was released, and was practically ignored by the large eastern dailies which control much of the nation's information flow.

On the agenda as speaker was James Forman, a civil rights leader prominent in the Student Non-Violent Coordinating Committee (SNCC) at the time of the 1965 Selma March and earlier. He had dropped out of the main spotlight when SNCC had undergone its Stokely Carmichael and H. Rap Brown periods, though Mr. Forman remained director of international affairs of the organization. He presented the Manifesto and called for a vote on it as the position of the development conference.

Mr. Forman wrote an introduction to the document, but who authored the rest of the Manifesto has not been announced. The vote itself became a matter of debate among those who did not attend the conference, particularly among those claiming Mr. Forman and the Manifesto had slim black support.

Over 500 persons were registered at the Detroit conference. The count on the Manifesto was 187 to 63. No rescinding action was taken, and Mr. Walker, conference chairman, later said it was considered an official statement of the meeting.

The aftermath made the vote a moot question. An NBEDC (later BEDC) steering committee was organized. IFCO board decisions turned it (or forced it) toward autonomy. Additional black churchmen were subsequently added to the committee. Mr. Forman became head of the Manifesto-demanded United Black Appeal, an idea for fund raising for the black community which had originated a year earlier with IFCO. He emerged as the spokesman and symbol of BEDC. (On the relation of IFCO to the NBEDC, the meeting, and on certain criticisms of the foundation, see Lucius Walker's "IFCO and the Crisis in American Society" in the Appendix.)

Mr. Forman was never president of BEDC, as some news reports indicated. There was no announced, official leadership until a gathering of the conference steering committee on July 11–13. Then, the Rev. Calvin B. Marshall, pastor of the Varick Memorial African Methodist Episcopal Zion Church of Brooklyn, was elected chairman. At that time, other executive officers and a slate of regional vice-chairmen were selected, and plans were made to seek legal incorporation. Mr. Marshall later noted that BEDC was far from a "paper organization."

Attempts to down-play Mr. Forman were rather persistent, sometimes from whites and again from blacks. On August 18, BEDC chairman Calvin Marshall categorically denied a report that Mr. Forman had been downgraded. Originating from newspaper misquotations from a Disciples of Christ clergyman, the story came shortly after an off-the-record BEDC program session held at a time when Mr. Forman was on vacation. In calling the report a "vicious, planted lie," Mr. Marshall noted that BEDC was a maturing organization and, as such, had no single spokesman. The Forman role in the BEDC and its United Black Appeal was vigorously defended. Mr. Marshall said Mr. Forman had turned down the chairmanship.

Albert Cleage, militant black pastor of a Detroit United Church of Christ, said in late June that strides toward black equality had changed, the new era being represented by BEDC and Mr. Forman. "You cannot make him (Forman) the stepchild," added Mr. Cleage. The Detroit clergyman was undoubtedly right, for many black leaders, religious and secular, endorsed the reparations principle. Notable among those condemning it were Bayard Rustin of the Randolph Institute, Dr. Jackson of the National Baptist Convention, U.S.A., Inc., and Bishop Stephen Spottswood of the AME Zion Church. Bishop Spottswood, also chairman of the board of directors of the National Association for the Advancement of Colored People (NAACP), felt reparations "easy and emotionally appealing, but not the fairest way for the white generation to redress the wrongs still visited upon this black generation and its children." He deemphasized the ideology of the Manifesto and called for alternative plans for black development.

The Connectional Council of the AME Zion Church, however, affirmed the concept of reparations in early August and asked the more than one million members to participate in BEDC. Among the public dissenters to the action was retired Bishop W. J. Walls of Chicago. Nonlegislating, the council is made up of bishops and heads of AME Zion agencies. Said a guideline statement to congregations: "We affirm the right of the black man to be. To be is to have power. To have power is to have self-determination. As the black man has been robbed of his power of being by a white racist society, it is incumbent upon that society to make restitution in order that there can be some meaningful reconciliation based upon diversity rather than conformity."

While reparations found much favor, all black spokesmen wholeheartedly approve the Manifesto programs or tactics. Mrs. Martin Luther King, Jr., speaking as an individual, found some merit in reparations but preferred massive church pressure on the government to worship disruptions. Southern Christian Leadership Conference officers were relatively silent for two months, some warming to reparations yet having too much to do in supporting a black hospital workers' strike in Charleston, S.C., to enter the BEDC-church controversy in the early months.

The Reverend Barnard Lee of SCLC endorsed church-paid reparations for hunger, better housing and correction of social ills, but not for guns, on June 29. Earlier, on June 21, Ralph David Abernathy, SCLC president, and Andrew Young, executive vice-president, did telegram an interesting message to R. H. Edwin Espy, general secretary of the National Council of Churches, on the eve of a session in which the executive committee of the ecumenical organization considered the Manifesto. The Manifesto was not endorsed in the wire, but a black challenge to white church "business as usual" could not be missed. They said:

> The Churches have long been guilty of a lack of stewardship in institutions. We have invested in profit-making corporations without concern that those profits came from exploitation of our brethren in southern Africa, Asia or Latin America. We have allowed God's treasure to be used to develop weapons of death and destruction. We have failed to invest in housing for the poor, jobs for the jobless, and given only a pittance to those instrumentalities which labor for peace and justice among men.
>
> Years ago, Truman Douglass [a late United Church of Christ leader], Eugene Carson Blake and Martin Luther King, Jr., each in his own way, issued a challenge about Christian stewardship over the tremendous investments of our Churches. Theirs was in reasoned, eloquent, and sound theological perspective, but their seeds fell on poor soil and took no roots.
>
> Now God has sent a crude but determined prophet to plague us to repentance, and we debate his language, his methods and ignore his message. There can be but one question to debate in regard to the so-called Black Manifesto: Is our Lord speaking to us through it? We black Christians have too often ignored the church and felt its power to be too limited or irrelevant in the principalities and powers of this age. Has God raised up this one from his own children of Abraham? These are questions to be discussed by men of faith, not a court of law. And if we discover that we are now the money changers in the Temple of our Lord, can we but confess our sins and determine the nature of our repentance? We pray for you in this hour of discernment.

Mr. Abernathy was in jail when the message was sent. He was seized while praying in the street. Others, not so often pictured on their knees, found more immediate recourse in the Manifesto. Roy Innis of the Congress of Racial Equality and George Wiley of the National Welfare Rights Organization borrowed the reparations approach in making demands on financial institutions and businesses. Spanish-American groups on the West Coast used it in appeals to churches. Demands, or plans for demands, were set by blacks in Boston, Detroit, Chicago, Indianapolis, St. Louis, Little Rock, Minneapolis and Los Angeles.

In mid-August Mr. Abernathy wrote in *The Christian Century* (August 15) that he first thought the NBEDC had gone too far in the Manifesto. He later came to see, he said, that before the reparations demands most "black Christians had given up on the church as a relevant institution with potential for social change." The SCLC head labeled Mr. Forman a "prophet to pull the covers off the economic life of the churches." Still, he did not see himself giving much time or energy to "pursuing the limited wealth of a lethargic church." Shortly thereafter, the SCLC announced major directional shifts which stressed work in black unionization and voter registration. Deemphasized were large national protests.

Without question the Manifesto Introduction is angry, revolutionary and somewhat socialistic. The text itself is more programmatic, asking the $500 million (or the three billion if the later figure is taken) for a wide variety of black projects. These include a southern land bank; four black printing facilities; four black television networks; a research center on black problems; a training center for instruction in community organization and communications; recognition of the National Welfare Rights Organization; a National Black Labor Strike and Defense Fund; International Black Appeal, African Liberation movements and a Black Anti-Defamation League, and for a black university in the South with greater flexibility in admissions than most schools practice.

The strategy for achieving the demands is straightforwardly disruptive of white church structures and ceremonies. While not drastically different from social legislation or proposals earlier made in the U.S., there is enough radical economics in the Manifesto itself to make the staunchly antisocialist uneasy. It threatens U.S.-style capitalism, accusing it of being oppressive to blacks.

Religious alignment with what is seen as an oppressive

system is the target of the Manifesto. The NBEDC's contention was that the religious groups themselves are large enough shareholders in the prevailing economic structure to come across with the sums demanded. The Manifesto does not tell the churches and synagogues how to collect the funds: digging deeper into pockets, liquidating assets or reordering programs for the sake of new priorities. Some specific presentations of "shares" did request breakdowns on holdings as well as percentages of income, in addition to set reparation amounts for IFCO or BEDC.

Admitting the shock impact, the concept of reparations in the Black Manifesto is not entirely foreign to the American experience. Literally, the verb form of the word "reparation" means "to mend" or "to amend." The Latin root also has connotations of "refresh" and "revive." In common political usage, however, "reparations" recalls the compensation Allied Powers required defeated Germany to pay after World War I and the United Nations handed Germany, Italy, Japan and Finland after World War II. Part of the purpose was to make the aggressors count the cost of the destruction caused. In such cases, and there have been others, reparations become extraction of funds or goods from a loser. This is not the sense in which the NBEDC used the word. U.S. blacks have scarcely been victors.

History, on the other hand, records situations where reparations have been paid to those who have suffered because of actions of a stronger or victorious nation, or of a majority. Though obtained from a loser, the $820 million Germany paid Israel for the resettlement of 500,000 Jews was reparations for political majority persecution. Israel was required to pay reparations to Arabs who lost homelands when the new state was set up in 1948. The U.S. knows of payment to damaged parties. Examples include government reimbursements to American Indian tribes whose land was illegally seized, to Japanese fishermen severely damaged from nuclear fallout from bombs tested in the South Pacific and insurance payments to families of servicemen killed.

Yet the term "reparation" is not normally applied to such payments in or by the nation. Partial explanation for the

limited use of the word is the implied guilt associated with it
by the international proceedings after the two world wars.
Americans are bothered by notions of collective guilt, as shown
by considerations of the subject following the Kerner Commission report. Theological reasons oppose affirmation of payment as a way to remove guilt. This was duly noted in various
rejections of the Manifesto. Unfortunately, the religious leadership was extremely slow in making theological appraisals of
reparations, generally responding first to the Manifesto's
rhetoric. Not undetected by blacks was the fact that white
churches pondered how reparations might fulfill justice without being a sponge for guilt only after they had rejected the
Manifesto's demands. In essays in this volume, several writers
raise some interesting points about reparations as ingredients
in worship and repentance.

Moreover, it must be mentioned that the Manifesto called
not for guilt but for action. The claim was put this way:

> For centuries we have been forced to live as colonized people
> inside the United States, victimized by the most vicious, racist
> system in the world. We have helped to build the most indus-
> trialized country in the world . . . We are also not unaware
> that the exploitation of colored peoples around the world is
> aided and abetted by white Christian churches and syna-
> gogues. This demand for $500 million is not an idle resolution
> or empty words. Fifteen dollars for every black brother and
> sister in the U.S. is only a beginning of the reparations due
> us as people who have been exploited and degraded, brutal-
> ized, killed and persecuted.

The Responses

Presentations of stipulated shares of the original $500 million
to religious groups, along with specific program emphases,
began at Riverside Church on May 4, though Mr. Forman
had on May 1 delivered the Manifesto to the Episcopal
Church and on May 2 to the policy-making General Board of
the National Council of Churches. Most delivery occasions
after Riverside in which Mr. Forman was involved were pre-
arranged. As the Manifesto movement spread around the

country, it was not always clear whether local groups—such as those carrying out Black Sunday church walk-ins in St. Louis—were acting unilaterally or in concert with the BEDC steering committee. That may be an irrelevant question since the Manifesto called on all blacks to consider themselves part of the conference.

By the end of July, demands in the name of the Manifesto had been made to the following national-level religious organizations: the National Council of Churches, the Episcopal Church, the Lutheran Church in America, the American Lutheran Church, the United Presbyterian General Assembly, the United Church of Christ, the United Methodist Board of Missions, the American Baptist Convention, the Christian Science Church, the Reformed Church in America and the Unitarian Universalist Association.

A demand for $200 million was handed to the Roman Catholic Archdiocese of New York, and separate presentations were made to Catholic prelates in other cities, such as Chicago and St. Louis. Geographic church conferences, synods and presbyteries, episcopal dioceses, area church groups, some seminaries and local congregations across the land also received demands. Interestingly, no Jewish agency or synagogue had been approached as of the end of August.

The total asked soon far exceeded $500 million. Not unpredictably, very little was forthcoming in grants, despite the many statements thanking God for the challenge. In mid-August the BEDC had received $1,000 from a black churchmen's group in Philadelphia, about $3,000 from students and faculty at Union Theological Seminary and $15,000 from the Washington Square United Methodist Church, New York; $500 each from informal Presbyterian and Catholic groups in Detroit and a pledge of a special collection for the United Black Appeal from the council of the North Side Cooperative Ministry in Chicago. The latter also voted $10,000 for black community use. Responses came from those receiving and not yet receiving demands. Most voiced strong concern over poverty and racism, though some of the avid conservatives clucked that the liberals were getting just reward for their social action involvement.

The Christian Century, the ecumenical weekly, seemed correct in its June 20 assessment that more attention was going to "the controversy over James Forman's representation . . . and the tension between a disruptive demand for social justice and the vindication of civil liberties such as the freedom of worship" than was being given "the crucial matter of economic analysis and public policy with regard to black poverty." The issue, said the *Century*, is "economic justice," the same conclusion reached by Mr. Abernathy and Mr. Young of SCLC. (Contrary to some press reports, the *Century* did not, however, endorse the Manifesto. In its July 2 issue, editors said that "to date, the Black Manifesto dispute has on both sides been an escape from such larger if less spectacular costs" for achieving economic justice, such as those set forth by the Kerner Commission.)

Leaving aside those who made no response, vast diversity marked the religious group responses, but in overview two patterns touching on religious economic aid to minorities emerged.

A—First is Manifesto rejection, usually with citation of already existing initiatives (or endorsement of some extant program), and expression of deep commitment to poverty eradication. This characterized reactions from the Catholic Archdioceses of New York and St. Louis, the Executive Council of the Episcopal Church, many Episcopal bishops in whose dioceses the matter arose, and United Methodist bishops, who noted a $20 million Fund for Reconciliation slowly being raised in the denomination.

(Also in this category between June 19 and June 30 was the administrative committee of the Executive Council of the United Church of Christ. On the latter date, a compromise response was adopted by the UCC's General Synod. An organization called Churchmen for Racial and Social Justice within the Church made demands which in many respects paralleled programs of the Manifesto. The synod revamped a Committee for Racial Justice into a Commission for Racial Justice, with a majority of the members to be black, and voted funds for the agency. It also approved feasibility studies on items such as a southern land bank, a black university, and black printing and publishing. This action put the United Church in type "B" response, but in the interim between June 19 and 30 it was a particular target for the kind of black criticism raised against type "A." This criticism is mentioned later.)

A variant on these reactions was Manifesto rejection which moved more directly to concern over poverty, leaving out listings of previous initiatives. Among these were the statements coming from the American Baptist Convention's executive unit, the southern Baptist Convention, the directors of the Christian Science Church and the American Lutheran Church's Council (which later included $3.4 million for the national crisis in its budget). Religious groups both receiving and not formally receiving the Manifesto fell into this category. The idea of reparations was generally disapproved.

Jewish agencies were specially inhospitable to reparations as an approach to black economic development, a factor noted as ironic by observers of several persuasions since Jews in modern history have received "financial amends." A joint statement of the Synagogue Council of America, representing all branches of American Judaism, and the National Jewish Community Relations Advisory Council, composed of most of the Jewish civic and humanitarian organizations, said: "It is evident that much remains to be done if the racial discrimination that has shamed our American past is to be wiped out. We believe that it is entirely in order for our religious and communal institutions . . . to be challenged, both from within and without, to face up to their shortcomings and responsibilities . . ."

But the joint statement, which served as basis of responses from rabbinical units and many Jewish leaders, found that "the demand for reparations . . . is not an answer to the inequities and injustices of our society." More "reliable" guides were identified as the Kerner Commission report, the Randolph Institute's "Freedom Budget" and the Urban League's "Domestic Marshall Plan." (Excerpts from the Jewish statement appear in the Appendix.)

Subsequently (action taken June 18 and disclosed June 30), the American Jewish Committee withdrew from IFCO. The crucial factor, according to Rabbi Marc Tanenbaum, former chairman of the IFCO board, was the foundation's "refusal to take a clear stand" as to where it stood on the ideology of the Manifesto, "with its call to guerrilla warfare and resort to arms to bring down the government." Plans were revealed for shaping twenty-three national Jewish groups into a coalition to give attention to social justice. IFCO was not ruled out as a funding agency, and respect for its achievements was voiced.

The Christian church responses which rejected the Manifesto expressed poverty concerns, and cited existing programs and proposals seemed to draw the most black ire, inside and outside the respective communions. They also won the most white support for BEDC. When on May 21 the New York Catholic Archdiocese turned hands down in one of the bluntest rejections, the Reverend J. Metz Rollins, a non-Catholic director of the ecumenical National Committee of Black Churchmen (NCBC), which has Catholic members, said the reply was an "almost absolute affront to the black church." (The demands to the Catholic Archdiocese of New York and the response are found in the Appendix.)

Commonweal, a Catholic weekly magazine, advised that the archdiocese could have done better than point to its charities and educational expenditures. The annual convention of the National Association of Laymen (Catholic) endorsed the principle of reparations. It asked an annual sum of $400 million from the U.S. Catholic Church for black-controlled organizations, requested a moratorium on church building except where structures serve the poor and urged the U.S. Catholic Bishops Conference to consider these proposals.

In Boston, an ad hoc white clergy group and the unofficial Association of Boston Urban Priests lent support to the Metropolitan Boston Committee of Black Churchmen in seeking $100 million from area religious groups, particularly the Christian Scientists. The priests' association said the churches and synagogues were the "logical starting point" in making reparations "to the black race for the centuries of systematic genocide (physical and psychological) that they have helped to force upon black people."

United Church of Christ rejection evoked the charges of evasion of the "cry of the black community" from Charles Cobb, director of that church's Committee for Racial Justice. A black churchman movement in the denomination expected that it would not be long until an interdenominational "convention of black Christians" could be formed. The church's biennial General Synod recommended its Board for Homeland Ministries to withdraw from a temporary restraining order against the BEDC sought by five agencies in New York's Interchurch Center, following incidents of "liberation." White leaders of the denomination, however, stressed displeasure with the Manifesto's philosophy, and the synod gave no funds to BEDC, though it did deal with demands from the black caucus in the denomination.

Episcopal Bishop Robert Emrich of Detroit declined to negotiate with BEDC representatives. In protest, eight white Episcopal women took over his office, saying they would stay until the bishop did agree.

B—Rejection (at least indirectly) of the Manifesto strategy and the BEDC as funding agent, but initiation—or offer to begin—some new program for black development was a second pattern. Taking this tack were Riverside Church, the United Methodist Board of Missions, the General Assembly of the United Presbyterian Church, the General Synod of the Reformed Church in America, the General Assembly of the Unitarian Universalist Association, Union Theological Seminary, New York, and the United Church of Christ (see above).

In general contrast to type "A" responses (with some local exceptions), each of these cases involved some disruption of normal functions or occupations of offices. Riverside's worship was interrupted; officers of United Methodist, United Presbyterian and United Church of Christ mission agencies were taken over, as were the general offices of the Reformed Church. The administrative wing of Union Seminary was "liberated" for twenty-four hours. Blacks walked out of the Unitarian meeting.

Further, four of the six sets of demands were initially linked to black members rather than directly to Mr. Forman. (This was also true of the American Lutheran Church and to numerous regional and local requests.) It was after a group of black Presbyterians seized the office of mission executive Kenneth Neigh that the BEDC spokesman was invited to address the United Presbyterian General Assembly. The United Methodist board was confronted by, and negotiated with, leaders of Black Methodists for Church Renewal. Union Seminary's entry into Manifesto developments was launched when black students and white colleagues issued financial demands to administrators and directors.

The BEDC strongly objected to decisions to fund black economic projects which entirely circumvented the conference. In early June, after the reparations issue had become a major church preoccupation, BEDC announced a drive to win formal recognition.

No two of the alternate programs were alike, and not all endorsed reparations, though the first official response to the Manifesto did. Ernest Campbell, preaching minister at Riverside Church, said, following consultation with the congregation's white and black leaders:

> Reparations, restitution, redress, call it what you will. We subscribe to the conviction that given the demeaning and heinous mistreatment that black people suffered in this country at the hands of white people in the slave economy, and given the lingering handicaps of that system that still work to keep the black man at a disadvantage in our society, it is just and reasonable that amends be made by many institutions in society—including, and perhaps specially, the church.

Riverside's plan was to "make a fixed percentage of its annual budget available to a fund to be set apart for the rapid development of all disadvantaged people in this country." (See the Appendix for the text of the Campbell statement.)

Union's trustees noted the imperative of "black economic development under black control." They voted to invest $500,000 in black enterprises in neighboring Harlem, to attempt to raise one million dollars to involve the institution in community projects, and the directors asked themselves to make personal gifts to a special fund to be administered by a committee made up of black students, faculty, alumni and directors.

Rejecting the "ideology, plans and tactics" of the Manifesto, the General Synod of the Reformed Church approved the formation of a denominational caucus of blacks—very few in that smaller denomination—to disburse a fund of at least $100,000 and coordinate new efforts toward meeting needs of minorities. Mr. Forman personally participated in an occupation of Reformed Church offices in New York and addressed the synod several days before the fund was voted.

Under synod mandate, black Reformed Church members formalized a Black Council in August. Rather than electing to disburse the $100,000, as the denomination proposed, the blacks rejected singularly responsibility for the fund and asked for greater participation in the policy-making executive and program units of the Church. The request pended November action by a Program Council.

Black Methodists for Church Renewal, a well-coordinated caucus successful in a number of program thrusts at the 1968 General Conference of the United Methodist Church, backed the reparation principle in mid-May. Members of that group and black employees of the Board of Missions made demands totalling more than one billion dollars of the New York-based agency. Included was $750,000 for BEDC. The executive committee of the board met on May 26, rejecting BEDC but proposing a possible $1.3 million for "economic empowerment" for blacks to be administered by six black bishops and board black personnel. Cain Felder, director of the black caucus, spurned the offer since it ignored BEDC. For various reasons, a majority of the black bishops reacted coolly to the task of overseeing such a fund. One noted that the Church had other structures—and maybe even the BEDC—for such work without coopting black bishops, who had as much to do already as white bishops. Another refused to have anything to do with what he felt were separatist approaches to black development.

In July, the General Assembly of the Unitarian Universalist Association was literally plagued by demands for attention to minority problems, the situation complicated by counterclaims of two groups within the association. A Black Affairs Council, administrative arm of a Black Unitarian Universalist

Caucus, won funding for its operations, to the displeasure of an integrated Unitarians and Universalists for Black and White Action. The former, aligned by personnel to the BEDC, also asked reinvestment of $5 million in programs outlined in the Black Manifesto, $1.5 million for other minorities and congregational reinvestment of $3.5 million in such work. The outcome was a substitute motion investing $1.6 million in projects with "high social value." Blacks withdrew the rest of the program in protest.

By far the most aggressive alternate program to the BEDC was that authorized by the United Presbyterian Assembly. The official statement on the national crisis did not employ the term "reparations." The denomination faced demands from the BEDC as well as from Spanish-American groups. Approved was a $50 million fund drive, proceeds to be used in "depressed areas and among deprived people." Mission units were instructed to give a total of $100,000 to IFCO and to continue in IFCO, supporting program possibilities "including those which develop as a result of the National Black Economic Development Conference." Steps were voted toward making church land usable by the poor, particularly in the Southwest, and $50,000 appropriated for cooperation with the Spanish-Americans.

Except for United Presbyterian action, all type "B" responses discussed above assigned—or attempted to assign—responsibility for black-directed economic development to some black denominational (or institutional) group. This tendency was also present on regional levels. For example, United Methodist conferences in New England, Missouri and Ohio voted large capital fund holdings or budget items to Black Methodists for Church Renewal. Blacks in Boston protested the failure to endorse reparations when the allocation was made.

Somewhat of a late-comer in the type "B" response was the Christian Church (Disciples of Christ). Since it did not receive formal BEDC demands, the Disciples situation is distinct from the examples above, at least in time and strategy dimensions. Early reactions from denominational leaders were mixed, recognizing the shock value of the Manifesto but voicing wariness over the rhetoric and source. Disciples president Doctor A. Dale Fiers opposed any National Council of Churches' concessions to BEDC but said officials of his Church would talk to Mr. Forman should he attend the mid-August General Assembly in Seattle.

Mr. Forman did not go to the meeting and there was little specific mention of the Manifesto in actions taken on racial-urban crises funding. The outcome, nonetheless, was tantamount to rejection of BEDC and the election of alternate, denominational approaches to fighting racism. To extend over a four-year period, the assembly approved strides to obtain $30 million of capital funds budgets—from agencies, congregations and national Church holdings—for minority-aiding efforts.

No doubt the initiatives were spurred in part by the vote a few days earlier in which a black Disciples unit voted to merge with the predominantly white assembly. An incipient black caucus was also active in Seattle. The Disciples, it must be stated, make what was probably the most honest confession of white religious complicity in the structures of racism of any church group which dealt with the Black Manifesto and its implications.

The BEDC was joined in late June by the National Committee of Black Churchmen (NCBC) in opposing alternatives to direct negotiation with and recognition of the Manifesto sponsors. Insistence by the ecumenical black caucus that BEDC be clearly recognized as representing black interests came to a head on June 23 as a result of action by the executive committee of the National Council of Churches, acting only on its own behalf. The committee was empowered by the council's policy-making general board to respond to the Manifesto. In so doing, the executive panel named a sixteen-member committee, including NCBC delegates, to consult with the BEDC, "to recommend program proposals for the NCC and to this end to consult with groups both within and outside the National Council."

NCBC leaders accused the council committee of walking "both sides of the fence" by refusing to recognize BEDC for fear of offending white constituents while still wanting to "pacify" blacks. NCBC declined to take part in the special committee until the National Council recognized BEDC, and until it asked the churches for $270,000 to organize the Manifesto group's administration and field services.

Apparently taken into account in BEDC and NCBC dealings with the National Council was the fact that the NCC is not structurally or financially a church. The council's endorsement and support seemed to be prized because of its broadly based representation. Both NCBC and BEDC boycotted the first meeting of the special committee, which was attended by four black delegates from NCC member churches. Out of the committee came a recommendation to the executive committee that the restraining order against Mr. Forman be withdrawn (as it was), and other measures affirmative of the legitimacy of BEDC as representative of black interests. On July 14 the executive unit met (Mr. Forman and other BEDC leaders were invited for part of the deliberations), but no agreement could be reached. Consultations were continued, with another executive session set for the late Summer or early Fall.

Cognizance of the nonlegislating role of ecumenical councils was reflected in a Black Manifesto encounter with a World Council of Churches consultation on the church and racism held in London in mid-May. Interrupting a session, BEDC participants asked $70 million. Eugene Carson Blake later said the group seemed to know the world council had no such funds and was therefore addressing the request to the 235 Protestant and Orthodox members around the world. Reparation was a major topic at the London meeting, with no thorough consensus found. Proceedings bore out the global dimensions of racism's challenge, a point made in the Manifesto. A list of recommendations to the world council's governing body did urge the churches to support and encourage reparations for all exploited peoples and to pressure governments to promote justice. Revolution as a last resort in the fight against racism was held to be justifiable.

The consultation's proposals did not, however, win the approval of the WCC's policy-making Central Committee in late August. The reparations principle was considered too close to inherited guilt and too lacking in compassion. The World

Council committee, after much haggling, formed a secretariat on racism with a $150,000 budget, and set aside $200,000 reserve funds for non-related groups working with oppressed people, if said groups were not outside the "general purposes" of the ecumenical movement. Member denominations were asked to give $300,000 more. Thus, the World Council gave a type "B" response by setting up an alternative program to BEDC.

Between May 4 and the end of the summer convention season, the only BEDC encounter with a church which was not stormy at some point was with the 67,000-member Evangelical Covenant Church of America at its annual meeting in Chicago. Henry Holmes, then mid-West director of BEDC, explained the Manifesto. No demands were made. Before the presentation the small denomination voted $67,000 per year each year until $335,000 was raised for black and poverty programs. Projects were to be selected by a committee of Black Covenanters.

There were also other special situations. No demands were delivered to the Presbyterian Church, U.S., its annual meeting having taken place before the matter of reparations arose. Various leaders and units within that denomination, nevertheless, made statements, the point of view generally being that the Manifesto could neither be wholly endorsed nor rejected.

No direct BEDC demands were made to the biennial convention of the Lutheran Church Missouri Synod, held in July. A group of blacks within that Church asked for greater attention to black schools operated by the synod and for concrete action to alleviate hunger. The reaction was primarily positive, with compliance felt possible out of general budget funds.

A proposal first made by the Disciples of Christ and echoed at the General Synod of the United Church of Christ for a national ecumenical meeting on black development received substantial backing. Not all black leaders, however, felt that details of such an event could be worked out by the white structures before late in the year. J. Metz Rollins, director of the National Committee of Black Churchmen, advised that nothing significant could come from another talk-fest. He urged a working conference.

Many individual churchmen and some groups—usually ad hoc—endorsed the reparations demands as just means of compensating for past discrimination against blacks. But, for the most part, official responses of churches measure from cool to negative. Theological reasoning and financial trepidation were both prime reasons. These arguments may not be without merit. On an acutely pragmatic level, however, highly informed persons have had possible reason to wonder if religious groups have been hypocritical in their rejection of reparations. This concerns the attitude to restitution payments in the past when religious organizations were on the receiving end.

Following World War II, scores of religious and charitable institutions filed, under a 1948 federal act, to recover losses resulting from the global conflict. It should be clearly understood that "reparations" were not asked. The term is "war claim," applying to property or other holdings seized or destroyed. The claimants collected, at least they got a portion of the askings. In many cases this was $10,000 plus 61.3 percent over the base sum. About 20 religious organizations—Protestant denominations, Catholic orders or societies, Jewish agencies and ecumenical projects—collected upwards of $14 million.

It was no doubt just for such restitution to be made. Where did the money come from? According to reliable sources, it came from reparations paid to the U.S. government by Germany. Reportedly, the specific money used for war claims was derived from the sale of a German chemical company. Churches whose top officials have been very cool to the BEDC's demands received in the millions of dollars in war claims payments. Examples include the forerunners of both the United Methodist and United Presbyterian Churches. In all fairness, it must said that such receipts were frequently spent for humanitarian purposes. The difference between $14 million and $500 million must also be seen. But there is more to the story.

Currently, a Coordinating Council of Religious and Welfare Agencies with War Damage Awards is seeking to win U.S. congressional approval for additional payments. Why? The religious and welfare recipients did not receive 100 percent of their claims. Death and personal injury and small business claimants did. The coordinating council is trying to persuade Congress to deal with religious awards under the small business category. On January 9, 1969, and February 7, 1969, bills to this effect were introduced, respectively, into the House of Representatives and the Senate. Similar measures had been introduced but not passed in former years. The present House bill is numbered 2669. The Senate bill is numbered 941. Should the request be granted by Congress, religious and charitable claimants would share some $5 million.

To reiterate, war claims paid to national groups by a government which received reparations is not identical to church reparations to blacks. Yet the principles involved cannot be divorced. Restitution is inescapably involved. If after 24 years, U.S. religious groups still feel entitled to payment for World War II losses, perhaps blacks may justifiably ask churches and synagogues to listen attentively to cries for restitution following four centuries of oppression which involved direct and indirect loss. Perhaps they have a right to demand payment. At least, the war awards raise some basic questions about the balance of religious institution's actions and ideologies.

Could the Churches Pay Reparations?

Polarization between whites and blacks in U.S. society increased over the Manifesto. Fuel was poured on hot coals when a West Coast police officer alleged that IFCO mainly funded militant and disruptive community groups; he made other unsubstantiated charges about secrecy in IFCO operations. Such charges, along with the BEDC-birth, unnerved IFCO church participants. Threats of ACTION, a St. Louis black organization, that it would spit in the communion cup unless demands to the Catholic Archdiocese were met did not win friends for the reparations cause. Tension—potentially creative, potentially disruptive—grew.

Significant disagreement between Manifesto supporters and ecclesiastical establishments involved religion's ability to pay reparations. A widely held white claim has been the unavailbility of access to such large sums. Bishop Emrich of Detroit summed up considerable white church reaction. He wrote that his first reaction to a Manifesto demand for $10 million from his diocese would be "to roll on the floor with laughter." BEDC postulated enormous religious wealth, an assertion which in the Manifesto responses received philosophical refutation but rather nonspecific analysis.

Could, or can, the churches and religious agencies of the nation provide the kind of money demanded? The question is probably unanswerable and, therefore, can be answered both ways, depending on the point of view. The most recent solid study, including a probe into the size of church wealth, is D. B. Robertson's *Should Churches Be Taxed?* (Westminster Press, 1968). The author concludes that total valuation of church property, holdings and revenues are, at best, estimates. He observes that many denominations honestly say they have no idea what they are worth. Perhaps this is among the reasons why Manifesto responders did not elect to issue tabulations of assets, as the BEDC asked. Other churches, Robertson noted, have a policy against making assets public.

Religion's revenues and holdings are, of course, substantial. The American Association of Fund-Raising Councils, Inc., reported that in 1967 46.9 percent of the $14,569 million contributed to philanthropic causes went to religion. A United Press International study released in Summer 1967 estimated church property value at about $100 billion. The figure may or may not be correct. It was the total used in late July, 1969 by Doctor Arthur S. Flemming, president of the National Council of Churches, for total church assets. (Doctor Flemming, former U.S. Secretary of Health, Education and Welfare, also suggested that the sum was large enough so that churches could give blacks $300 to $500 million for welfare projects.) The problem of obtaining a total and accurate figure of church-religious economic power is hardly dependent on willingness or unwillingness to publicize the information. Unwillingness may frequently be the case, but other matters are involved. Religious denominations, orders and agencies are usually not centralized. Varying state laws apply to holdings. Congregations, dioceses, synods, boards and commissions have debts as well as assets. The stock market goes up and down. A thorough computation of the financial ins and outs of religion would require a data-gathering and bookkeeping system not yet developed in the nation.

Furthermore, while religious units frequently have large stock holdings and investment portfolios, contributions remain the cornerstone of financial operations. And in recent years, giving to top program-making echelons has either leveled off or been cut back. A partial explanation is congregational need for more money to implement local priorities in education and social action. The liberal stances of many national religious groups on social issues has also taken its toll among more conservative givers.

Alas, it is honestly the situation that many religious organizations have more paper than actual wealth. For example, the United Methodist Church has official ties with scores of educational institutions, hospitals, orphanages, homes for the aging, camps and assembly grounds. The value of these properties would be included in any total assessment of the denomination's wealth. But the Church probably could not legally dispose of these holdings to obtain funds for other works, even if buyers could be found. Rather than being assets in terms of income, most are liabilities.

Shortly after it received Manifesto demands, the New York Catholic Archdiocese published figures showing a possible $30 million deficit in its parochial school system by 1972. A report said that per capita giving at Sunday Masses rose 45 percent between 1958 and 1964 but rose only 6.9 percent between 1964 and 1967. No drop in giving is indicated, but a decrease in percent of increase is enough to make church budgeters cautious in the face of rising prices for goods and services. The archdiocese also told of a $1.2 million deficit in 1968. It was the first financial report released.

At Riverside Church, a sizeable endowment is almost entirely limited by charter to the upkeep of a nearly two-block-square building. To its credit, that congregation does utilize the space fairly constantly. Frequently, local churches find themselves paying large proportions of budgets to maintain a structure used only once a week and far too large for current attendance.

On the other hand, church-launched foundations—not ranking with Ford but holding millions—might utilize interest or principal for paying reparations. Enormous church stock caches exist, the income used to fund programs or held for a "rainy day." In some minds the flood is about up to the roof, and time to redeem the chips is overdue. Reluctance to do so may be economically prudent if not religiously faithful. Religious groups also own manufacturing firms and rental property: the extent of such involvement is slowly leaking out as government and churches themselves look into tax structures.

Without doubt, the organized religious bodies *could* pay $500 million and more in reparations. They might be forced to retrench in other program spheres. Parochial schools as traditionally operated might have to be curtailed or discontinued, foreign missions limited, meetings pared down and agency staffs trimmed. They would most certainly lose contributions. Religious bodies as they exist *could*, with effort, raise $500 million. To do it might well destroy their normal, relatively comfortable shapes.

Destruction of the churches does not seem to be the motive of the BEDC. During an hour on the "Night Call" radio dialogue program, Mr. Forman took care to point out that church and synagogue members as well as official administrative units were asked to pay reparation. Businessmen who comprise the trust boards of religious institutions were especially tagged as responsible for black economic development. Such optimism may anticipate a life-surge instead of a death-wish. Mr. Forman obviously takes the churches as totalities of members more seriously than religious leaders, who may be the more realistic. Churchmen know neither they nor delegated assemblies have the power to extract funds from members for any cause. At most, moral authority resides in a church statement or request, and only when constituents have agreed to that authority.

When the BEDC is funded from any source and whether reparations is the device selected for speeding black economic development, may be secondary to the goal of economic justice. In 1969, the action is with reparations and it could stay there. It is somewhat amazing that organized religion has a chance—in a supposedly secular age—to get a firm hand on the wedge opening the door to the future. Religion's future, more than BEDC's or black development's, is at stake as it deals with racism and reparations. The Black Manifesto was not wrong when it said of the churches and synagogues: ". . . their faith and belief in the Cross and the words of the prophets will certainly be put to a test. . . ."

New York City
Fast of Ab, July 24, 1969

CONTROL, CONFLICT AND CHANGE
The Underlying Concepts of the Black Manifesto

by JAMES FORMAN
Chairman, United Black Appeal

ON SATURDAY, April 26, 1969, in Detroit, Michigan at a Black Economic Development Conference sponsored by the Inter-religious Foundation for Community Organization (IFCO), we issued the Black Manifesto which is basically divided into three parts: (1) the preamble, a prophetic version of how we see change and revolution inside the United States; (2) concrete programs and demands for reparations upon the racist white, Christian churches and Jewish synagogues; (3) programmatic ways or tactics to achieve our objectives.

Since the issuing of the Black Manifesto many of us have spoken throughout the United States trying to organize support for its implementation. The following article is written primarily for Black Dialogue, but it is fundamentally the speech I delivered at the National Black Theatre on Sunday, July 6, 1969. The spoken word has been adapted to a written style in some instances. It is the intention of the author that this article and "speech" will form a supplement to the Black Manifesto and that a minimum of seven million copies will be distributed in black communities throughout the United States. The international implication of the Manifesto is evidenced by the fact that the Political Bureau of the Republic of Guinea has issued an editorial of support.

Inside the United States we suffer from the most vicious, racist, capitalistic, imperialistic system known to mankind. Whereas all of us in this room today, at this particular gathering of the National Black Theater, may be struggling for our liberation, there are millions of black people who are not struggling for their liberation, who are not totally conscious of all their oppression.

Why is this the case?

Why is it that some of us are dedicated to giving our total lives for the liberation of black people and others are not? The answer lies fundamentally in the mass line of the BEDC and its Black Manifesto; namely the three "c's": control, conflict and change.

Operating upon all of us are a whole set of control factors, many of which we are not aware. These control factors, however, have been drummed in our heads for centuries, and we accept them as realities, hence the major reason we are not all totally dedicated to liberation.

It is not enough just to say that the system is tyrannical; that it's racist; that it's capitalistic; that it's imperialistic. Although that is a correct analysis, what are some of the manifestations of racism, capitalism and imperialism that make us submit to tyranny inside this country? This can be determined by a thorough discussion of the control factors operating on our lives.

Any kind of liberation struggle—anywhere in the world— seeking revolution, intending to overthrow oppression, trying to deal with the tyranny that oppresses that particular group of people *must*, in fact, make this concrete analysis of all of the control factors operating upon that oppressed group of individuals.

Inside the United States there are approximately thirty major control factors operating upon us. In every city, in every town, in every county and in every state there will be additional variations; but what we are talking about are the major control factors which make us submit to the tyranny of this country. These kinds of control factors are responsible for our brothers fighting in Vietnam; *they are not mercenaries.* We have been so indoctrinated, so controlled by certain factors as we grow up that we begin to fight in Vietnam for the United States government, even though there are those of us who are opposed to fighting in Vietnam.

What are some of these control factors?

One: *The concept of citizenship*. This is a major control factor. The entire fabric of this particular system of government is designed to instill in us the concept that we are citizens of this country. Every particular act of the various institutions inside the United States tries to drum this into our minds every day.

We know this concept of citizenship is a lot of bull.

We know that.

We're hipped to that.

We were not citizens in 1789 when they said we were three-fifths of men as written in the Constitution of the United States.

We're hipped to the fact that we are not citizens today. Nevertheless, it is imperative that this government try to consciously promote the feeling that we are citizens of this country. It is only by promoting the concept that we are citizens of this country that it is able to control us and make us submit to its tyranny. Therefore, one of the first jobs that we have to do is to work to consciously destroy the myth that we are citizens of the United States.

Two: *The educational process*. The educational process of the United States is geared not only to make us feel that we are citizens, but also to make us conform. It is geared to make us super patriots, geared to make us obey the police, obey the courts and all other institutions of this false democracy. Therefore any liberation struggle *has* to deal with the educational process inside a colonized territory, inside any situation where people are oppressed. We know this. All we have to do is to open our eyes and look at the educational system inside the United States. That educational system does not teach us to rebel against the United States, but in fact teaches us how to conform. A classic example is how we all learn to place our hands on our hearts and recite: "I pledge allegiance to the flag of the United States of America and to the Republic for which it stands, one Nation under God, indivisible, with liberty and justice for all." For eight years in elementary school we say it. This is a conscious inculcation, a conscious brainwashing by the educational system.

Check the textbooks; check the history books.

When we get into high school, we notice brothers in the Reserve Officer Training Corps (ROTC) saluting and reciting once again: "I pledge allegiance to the flag of the United States of America...." By the time a brother is eighteen, the educational system has consistently programmed him where he wants to become a Second Lieutenant in the United States Air Force or in the United States Army. That is why ROTC exists in colleges—to reinforce the primary and secondary educational system which makes us submit to this kind of government.

Three: *The mass media and the communication system.* This is fundamentally a technique of the United States and all Western powers with their highly industrialized communication systems. It's no accident that many of the so-called "Negro" newspapers in this country are in fact owned by white capitalists. What goes into those newspapers affects our images—not to mention the *New York Daily News* and all the garbage which is spread throughout the United States.

The psychological control effect of the television network in this country has never really been estimated. We know it's there, notwithstanding "Julia." It's no accident that the "Black Heritage" program was shown at 9:00 o'clock in the morning. This was a deliberate programming, in order not to get the ideas contained in "Black Heritage" over to the masses of black people. At 9:00 o'clock in the morning we are out hustling jobs, and we don't have time to turn on the television.

Four: *The dogma and practice of the white Christian churches.* As far as I'm concerned, this has been one of the most consistent and effective control mechanisms operating upon us. I happen to be old enough to remember my mother telling me: "Well, don't worry about the white man, son; he'll get his in hell. We will have everlasting life, so don't worry about him; these 60 or 70 years of hard times which we face will be nothing compared to our eternity of peace and his eternity of damnation." As long as this kind of psychology and ideology is spread by the Christian churches, people will not go on to struggle for their liberation.

During the period of slavery and even today in most instances the practices and dogma of the Christian churches are in fact made to order for an enslaved group of people. Let us examine it: Here we are slaves inside the United States, and so the man comes with the Bible and says "Blessed are the poor, for they shall inherit the earth, or they shall see God. Blessed are the meek for they shall see the kingdom of God." Here we are poor—toiling in the fields, chopping the cotton and the man says to us, "It is easier for a camel to go through the eye of a needle, than it is for a rich man to go to heaven."

So all of these things were comforting in many ways to our ancestors and even to some of us. Now I don't take the position—and this is something that we have to argue about—that the Christian church was in fact a survival element for black people. That's just a hypothetical argument. We have no way of proving it; but I do know that the ideology, practices, and involvement with the Christian church helped to control us and made us submit more and more to the tyranny of this country.

Now the same thing is true today because many people believe the racist Christian ideology, believe that there is an eternity, believe there is life after death, that God is all powerful and that even the sufferings on this particular earth will be rewarded by eternity.

Five: *The profit motive system and upward mobility*. The system strives to make us competitive. If we are not competitive, we cannot become good capitalists. We cannot become good people inside this system of government, and we are programmed consciously to try to make money, to make profits, to be upward mobile, to try to get more and more cars, a better home; and all that's on an individualistic basis too.

Six: *The love of life and the fear of death*. This is very real, you see, because this society with its materialistic base makes us want to love life, makes us want to love life consciously. We are supposed to love life and fear death and that becomes a very significant control mechanism. It is better to die at 19, struggling to be a human being, *struggling to be a man, struggling to be a woman* than to die of old age enduring all sorts of oppression throughout our lives.

The love of life becomes real because many people are not

willing to take chances, are not willing to risk, are not willing to make sacrifices, are not willing to do day-to-day work because they love life, and they fear death. They don't want to be killed; they want to live. And, therefore, they will submit to all forms of tyranny and oppression because they want to live; and there is only one absolute certainty in life, and that's death. Once you're dead, you're dead; there's no reprieve, no redress, no heaven, no hell. You are dead, and if you lie out on the streets, you'll rot away. And you will see what there is afterwards. It doesn't matter how much embalming fluid, or what type of caskets we get, death is death! If we, in fact, fear death and we are not willing to take certain risks, then we will stay oppressed.

This is a problem that the Vietnamese also face. To love life is a part of Western mythology. One is supposed to love life despite all of the bad things inherent in Western civilization which go on. And I maintain that the love of life and fear of death is a key control factor. We should not allow the fear of death to operate as a control mechanism even though we do.

Seven: *The fear of ideologies which call for revolution in the United States.* This is another mechanism which the man uses to control us. There is no mystery why the Panthers are being attacked. There is no mystery why brothers who espouse liberation or revolution are in jail all over this country. The man, the government, wants to make us fear these kinds of ideologies. There is no mystery, even as far as the BEDC is concerned, why there is a federal grand jury subpoenaing people in Detroit, Michigan like today, and the BEDC is only two months old. But the federal government has seen fit to call the grand jury hearing to subpoena people. Now ask yourself, why? Obviously, if it were no threat, there would be no federal grand jury. Check it out. Look around, there are a whole lot of people who are walking around doing one thing and saying another. But they are not being persecuted by the government. In many ways, they don't pose as great a threat as do other forces and other individuals. You can judge the effectiveness of some things by the amount of persecution which the government puts down. If you are not a threat, they will not bother you; they'll just let you run around. That's a fact.

Eight: *The police and other military forces.* Ordinarily, when we think of control, this is what we think of as a major force; but it's not. All of these other factors we have talked about are important because the police can't be everywhere. The police cannot be all over Africa. The military alone did not control Africa. It took the missionary, money, indirect rule and other aspects of colonialism. The police and the military are one of the last control mechanisms any government uses. Sometimes we make the mistake and just think the police are the only control mechanism operating on us, and if we did away with the police that would end our problems. This is just not true.

Nine: *The administration of justice, the courts, bail, the judicial system.* It's no wonder that the brothers who were arrested in the so-called Panther plot have a $100,000 bail on them, or that there were various legal entanglements in the so-called July 21, 1967, "frame-up." All of the administration of justice becomes a control mechanism because, if you impose high bail, then the brothers can't get out on the streets. If the juries are stacked, there is no chance for justice.

Ten: *The use of police informers, spies, rumors and slander campaigns.* In certain black communities it is said the spy network is greater than the CIA overseas. That's possible and real. Look at the history of frame-ups here in Harlem. Look at the so-called Statue of Liberty case, where Woods, a police informer, began to set up the whole plot, went and got the dynamite and planted the microphone in the brother's car; and Woods is still running around. He might be informing on this meeting, I don't know.

Many of the brothers who are fighting for liberation in Rhodesia say that there are so many police informers spying for the Ian Smith government that any time they try to mount an attack in any particular city or countryside that the brothers go and fail. Police informers have framed most of the militants who have been unjustly accused of certain so-called crimes. The case of Brother Ferguson is only one recent example. Ironically, the government is using black people to in-form on one another, and some of us fall for this treachery for a few pieces of silver.

I assure you there is only way to deal with police informers and you know what I mean. I want to make this very, very clear; we've said this all over the country and I'm saying it right here. Now you can call that hot air if you want to, or you can call it just a lot of wolfing, but you take your chances, because there is only one way in the world we are going to stop these informers from standing up.

Eleven: *The assassination of black leaders.* The killing of people who take frontal positions against the injustices of this society, who fight racism, capitalism and imperialism and who refuse to submit to the tyranny of this country is a mechanism that the government uses to control the rebelling black population. In Cleveland today Brother Ahmed Evans is facing electrocution. The government is finding a scapegoat for the July 23, 1968, self-defense in Cleveland. Brother Ahmed Evans is absolutely innocent, and I am told by Sister Mae Mallory that the record indicates he was in the house of a police officer for six hours during the whole time of rebellion. However, since there was a strong military apparatus developing among the brothers, the state of Ohio and the United States government are deliberately assassinating this brother to help control the population. All of us who are black must join in the fight to save his life and unite with the July 23rd Defense Committee which is fighting for his survival.

But the most effective method of curbing some of the assassinations of black leaders is to organize for retribution. That retribution has to be deliberately planned, well organized and quite selective. No man can protect his life ultimately. There is a picture to our left of Brother Malcolm who paid the supreme price, but is no accident that he was killed in public. His killing was designed by the CIA to frighten the population as it did in many instances. All those lynchings from the period of Reconstruction through today were inflicted upon black men and women to frighten the population, to make all of us afraid to challenge the system of government that oppresses us. The will of a people is weakened to the degree that it is frightened by the assassination of its leaders.

When we were working to save the life of Brother Huey, we raised the cry that the sky is the limit if he were sent to the electric chair. Some of us were prepared to go down if he had been killed by the state, for only organized, deliberate and selective retribution will minimize the killing of black people by the corrupt military machinery of this government. Political leadership must establish its price well in advance of its assassination. It must call for the destruction of power stations, gas outlets, police stations, water pumps and buildings, and the selective killing of imperialists who are choking the life of mankind around the world. As the struggle escalates, the price must go higher and higher; and organization for retribution and revolution must become more deliberate, more scientific, carefully planned and intensely selective.

Efforts must be made to organize all segments of the population. Forms of organization and stages of struggle cannot be skipped, for the final clash is years away and probably will not come in our lifetime, but we must work as if every day is the final day—taking the long-range viewpoint so as not to become frustrated and demoralized when quick victories are not around the corner.

Twelve: *The lack of job security, inadequate payment of wages, and consumer credit.* The ability to deny one security for his family and for himself through the withholding of wages and the dismissal from his or her job becomes one of the most effective control mechanisms that this society imposes upon us. Wage payments and consumer credit are designed to effectively control the population and make us all toe the line of the capitalist road to destruction. Many people do not struggle for fear of losing their jobs and the meager security they have for their family. Consumer credit and the installment plan of buying has been the graveyard of many militants and potential revolutionaries, for we are programmed to want goods and services more than justice and liberation.

Thirteen: *The practices of the white-dominated trade unions.* Trade unions in this country are not only racists in their treatment of black workers, union practices and officer structure, but also in terms of their practices and attitudes toward the third world, the people of Africa, Asia and Latin America.

General Motors, Ford, Chrysler and all the other automotive industries are locating in South Africa, for instance; but at the same time the racist United Automobile Workers' Union does not call a strike against these plants for their treatment of black workers in South Africa, or the miserable wages or policies of apartheid.

Black workers in many parts of this country form sixty-five to eighty percent of the work force at the point of production, but they do not control their unions; and the racist white-dominated leadership has no interest in ending their exploitation or that of black people around the world.

Fourteen: *The denial of adequate health and medical facilities.* The infant mortality rate is so high for black infants that genocide is committed at birth. If black children cannot grow up to be men and women, their potential for revolutionary work is killed by the state. There is no medical school in Harlem or many other black communities by deliberate calculations of the racist government of the United States.

While it is true that thirty to fifty million of us survived the atrocities of the slave trade, how many of us died and do die through the lack of adequate medical facilities? Clearly inadequate medical facilities is a form of genocide.

Fifteen: *The welfare system and its administration.* This is self-explanatory.

Sixteen: *Dope in our communities.* When young black men and women thirteen and fourteen years old are addicted to heroin and never live to see sixteen, how can they fight to liberation? It is impossible. In fact, they become agents against liberation when they become twenty-two or twenty-three because they are forced to rob the population in order to get dope. The Mafia is a third government inside the United States. While the black dope pusher is part of this control mechanism, he is still not the major source. He is a minor agent, for the real responsibility lies with the system of government that allows it to come across the borders, profits in it and allows it to flourish in black communities.

Seventeen: *The downgrading of our African heritage and culture.* This is a factor we are all aware of. But to the extent we accept and upift Western history, Western values, Western culture, Western mythology, Western religion, the process of control becomes more effective.

Eighteen: *The lack of concrete ties with the African continent.* The importance of this as a control mechanism can be more readily understood by comparing the situation of the Jews in this country to Israel as a state. The United Jewish Appeal and other forms of Jewish philanthropy inside the United States had much to do with the financing of militant Jewish groups and the formation of Israel.

Our own consciousness about helping African liberation movements is not very developed, and there are few ways in which we lend our technical skill to develop the African continent. This in turn forces African countries to turn to their former colonial masters and even to Israel for help. I am not suggesting the fault is entirely ours, but we must accept our share of the responsibility. The fault is fundamentally with imperialism, but we must try through our own efforts to break it.

In Tanzania, for instance, Israel built a hotel which will be completely owned by the Tanzanian government in a few years. Yet, once the hotel was built, it was necessary for the Tanzanian government to send some of its citizens to Israel to study bed making, the art of waiting tables, cashiering and other trades associated with the running of a hotel. Tanzania exercised its options, but these are skills which we employ and teach every day.

SNCC (Student Nonviolent Coordinating Committee) once tried to have a program called the Afro-American Skills Bank through which we would try to send people from the United States to Africa for a period of two or three years, and we got very high confirmation from African governments. Obviously, the Central Intelligence Agency and the entire fabric of the United States government moved to stop this program through various means. It would have been too much of a threat to this government for black people to go abroad, not under the sponsorship of the United States government, but actively carrying a line that is opposed to this form of government.

The lack of concrete ties with the African continent makes

it possible for our continent to be exploited by others; and it strengthens the possibilities for lies by the United States government and dissension between Africans on the continent and those of us overseas, including our brothers and sisters in the West Indies. For instance, the United States Information Agency prints a magazine called *Topic* which is distributed only in Africa. In the first issue it showed Bob Moses and Mrs. Fannie Lou Hamer winning two seats at the Democratic convention of August, 1964. This is a flagrant lie, but it was told by a government that is engaged in coups and killings to get its will, and the telling of a lie in Africa is not beyond its capacity. The United States government had to explain what happened at the Democratic convention of 1964, and it chose to lie about the results, for the truth would have been damaging to its propaganda. Other issues of this magazine have showed the Bronx High School of Science with a high percentage of blacks. They are trying to promote the concept that integration is an American dream which becomes a reality in that high school. One issue stated that the average income of all blacks in the United States is $7,000 a year.

Through the lack of concrete ties, the U.S. government is able to program us and Africans into believing there is no solidarity between the two of us to intensify the propaganda that upward mobility is a virtue which all blacks in the U.S. seek as well as the material possessions of this country. Inside Africa, the Cultural Affairs officers of the U.S. embassies have the greatest contact with the African masses; and most, if not all, of these are "Negroes" who help to spread rumors and false information about our condition in the U.S.

Nineteen: *The domination of the African continent by the Western powers.* As long as the African continent is dominated by Western economic interests, then we can expect little help from it in our fight for liberation. Nobody will stand up in the United Nations and champion the cause of black people inside the U.S. if there is great fear of economic retaliation by the U.S. and other Western interests. It is no accident that it is difficult to find countries in Africa that will assist a brother who is seeking political asylum. There are some, but their numbers are limited; and this relates to the precarious economic position in which the African countries find themselves, although we must learn to live underground inside the U.S. We ourselves must realize that we are much to blame for these conditions for we have not heightened our own sense of consciousness and concrete work to help eliminate these conditions. At the same time black CIA agents, cultural affairs officers, other representatives of the U.S. government do much —deliberately—to antagonize the African population with respect to us living in the U.S.

Twenty: *The lack of capital for the cooperative development of black communities in this country and Africa.* This is an extremely vicious obstacle and control mechanism. For while Africa is the richest continent on the earth, yet it is very poor. In order to develop industrially, capital is needed. Colonial powers granted political independence but maintained control of most economies. There is no mystery why Brother Nkrumah didn't survive, for he was on the verge of breaking the stranglehold on the Ghanian economy imposed by the Western powers. The lack of funds for the cooperative development of the black community results from the intense profit motive system under which we live and the desire to maintain that system.

Twenty-one: *The lack of organizations which seek to develop political, economic and military forms for the survival and revolution.* Many organizations relate to only one side of the triangle—the political, military, economic triangle—but all organizations should seek to develop the three simultaneously. During the period of Reconstruction, there were many forms of political activity by black people, but the inability to defend the black political institutions caused their loss as well as the loss of the lives of many people. The political ideology must seek revolution with a cooperative economic content.

Twenty-two: *The absence of a centralized intelligence agency for the use of black people against their white oppressors, house niggers included.* This is vitally necessary to minimize informers, to post and spread information about good, bad and indifferent programs in the community. This requires a high degree of skill in running a security apparatus, but these skills can be acquired.

Twenty-three: *The lack of trained cadres capable of organizing people to struggle for their liberation.* Explaining and promoting struggle against the control factors operating upon us can only come through disciplined cadres agitating for their change. In Vietnam this is called armed propaganda units, but the form remains the same. There must be conscious, dedicated groups of people willing to make every sacrifice to promote conflict in order to produce change.

Twenty-four: *The promotion among black people that non-violence is the method to change our conditions inside the U.S.* At this stage of our struggle we can see how the government is intensely trying to cling to this concept while it plunders and kills in Vietnam.

Twenty-five: *The inability to understand that the total population, men, women, and children must be seen as revolutionary.* This is quite often difficult for some brothers who are not in the habit of realizing the revolutionary nature of women; but, if the Algerians had adopted this attitude, then their revolution would not have succeeded to the point it did; for the liberation front mobilized the total energies of the population, women included. Algerian women were very effective in concealing weapons and transporting messages.

Twenty-six: *The Poverty Program.* It was designed to control the rising militancy of the black population. There are some brothers and sisters within it trying to use it against the government, but for the most part revolutionary militancy has been curbed by the introduction of the poverty program in certain areas.

The poverty program and other federally funded projects are not designed to instill the habit of cooperative ownership, but to pay off and buy more stooges. One must wonder with all the money that the poverty program spends why there is not one major industrial printing plant where black people are learning the skills of industrial printing.

Twenty-seven: *Psychological warfare perpetrated by the U.S. government inside black communities.* The extent of this is not known, but we would be most unwise not to realize that a government that has trained personnel in psychological warfare operating around the world would not apply some of those same techniques inside an area it considered dangerous.

We mentioned rumors. There are those which get passed by the population in general, and there are those which get deliberately fostered and promoted by agencies of the government, especially the Central Intelligence Agency and the Federal Bureau of Investigation. Unfortunately, many people feel they can talk to the FBI without realizing that the FBI and the CIA play on percentage points. They will spread rumors in order to frighten the population.

Then there is the type of psychological warfare which tries to make us believe all the problems reside within us and that there are no external forces causing our oppression. Quite often this line is internalized by many of us. Therefore, we sometimes hear that there must be absolute unity before we can do anything, or that there are no class factors within the black community. The government achieves desired results if any segment of the population ignores the objective realities of the control forces operating upon it and rather believes that the fault is solely within it.

Twenty-eight: *Compacted living conditions and inadequate housing. Genocide.*

Twenty-nine: *The lack of land and the thievery of land.* Historically we have been cheated of land in this country. We worked the land; we made others rich. Not only was there no land redistribution after the Civil War, but there has been a systematic attempt to deprive black people of the little land they have owned through the years. But there is no reason for us to assume that any land anywhere in the U.S. does not belong to us. We have as much right to the land and resources of this country as anyone. There are some of us in the Black Economic Development Conference who assert the total land mass and resources of this country must be administered under revolutionary black leadership in order to prevent the recurrence of racism and exploitation.

Self-Determination and the Transfer of Power

Essentially, the fight for reparations is one of self-determination and the transfer of power. We have made demands upon one of the major sources of capital in this country. There are fundamentally only seven major sources of capital in the United States: The United States government, banks, business enterprises and corporations, foundations, churches and people. We have no argument with anyone demanding reparations from the U.S. government. We support their efforts, and we realize that the call for reparations is not a new one. However, the churches must be viewed as an extension of the government. Not to understand the two-thousand-year-old historical relation of the Christian church with the rise and fall of governments and their complicity in our enslavement is to miss a very important political point and the crux of our demand for reparations.

The Christian church and Jewish synagogues must not be seen merely as religious institutions. They are more than that. They are more than just a control mechanism with their ideology of servitude. The Christian churches and Jewish synagogues must be seen as financial giants operating in a new trinity—the church, business and government.

It is the unveiling and unmasking of the financial role of the church which is causing the greatest consternation, the greatest opposition. For the church has operated as a huge financial giant for many years in this country, and its power grows greater every day. The Catholic church is more than a powerful second government in many countries. It is a worldwide government with tremendous influence. The world missionaries of all the denominations work hand in hand with goverment and business.

The National Black Skills Bank. In order to more effectively deal with the program demands contained in the Manifesto, we are in the process of organizing throughout the United States the talents and skills of many black people into the National Black Skills Bank. We are encouraging the formation of these units so that the Manifesto may be adapted and expanded upon to fit the conditions of any given area. We do not claim that the projected sites listed in the Manifesto are fixed and immutable. We are asking people around the country to adapt them to their particular area and to help in their implementation. We are most concerned with the use of leisure time. Many people have free time after their job, and the use of this leisure time becomes very important. If many people would donate six to eight hours a week fighting one or more of the control mechanisms operating upon us, then we would be further ahead on the road to liberation.

Resistance to the Black Economic Development Conference. In the initial stages many people thought we were not serious. Our determination and our capacity for work began to force more recognition of our demands. Then there was an effort to completely circumvent us. In Harlem this took the form of the Union Theological Seminary agreeing to give $1,000,000 for cooperative development of the community but not to the Black Economic Development Conference. Who gets this money is yet to be decided. In addition, the Union Theological Seminary voted to give $500,000 to Harlem businessmen. This was basically unacceptable to us for we are not out to make any more black people capitalists, but to foster the cooperative economic development of communities.

Along with the efforts to circumvent us came the picking and choosing of certain "Negroes" with which to negotiate and deal. We fought and will fight the bypassing of our leadership. After the churches began to recognize we had more and more popular support, then they began to trot out certain "Negro" spokesmen and to have them to try to discredit our efforts. This has been coupled with a massive witch hunt by the Federal Bureau of Investigation and a federal grand jury hearing.

Conclusion.

Our demand for $500 million in reparations from the churches was an effort to break some of the control mechanisms operating upon us in some small way. We know that this effort is not a total solution to our problems, but the struggle we are making and will make around our demands will heighten our revoutionary consciousness; and the implementation of any one of our demands is an asset. However, more important than that is what we believe has been the new perception by many black people of power, its use, and how we may achieve more "on this earth." We have escalated our demands to three billion dollars because of the control the churches have on the southern "Negro" colleges. We have sought increased funds for them from all the denominations in order to try to make them truly black universities. While we do not envision a quick victory but years of sustained struggle, we are quite confident that conflict must be created around control mechanisms. This is not passive action. There must be a deliberate call to action, definite acts of defiance, concrete organizational forms, a positive assertion of the human will to struggle for revolution, "a will to decolonize," by whatever means available.

We urge your support and ask you to join in the struggle. Thank you!

REPARATIONS: REPENTANCE AS A NECESSITY TO RECONCILIATION

by WILLIAM STRINGFELLOW

And if ye shall perceive your offenses to be such as are not only against God, but also against your neighbors; then ye shall reconcile yourselves unto them; being ready to make restitution and satisfaction, according to the uttermost of your powers, for all injuries and wrongs by you to any other; and being likewise ready to forgive others who have offended you, as ye would have forgiveness of your offenses at God's hand; for otherwise the receiving of the holy Communion doth nothing else but increase your condemnation. —an exhortation or warning for the celebration of the Holy Communion in *The Book of Common Prayer*

THE REPARATIONS DEMAND of the National Black Economic Development Conference has been heard in the white churches and synagogues with a mixture of resentment and dismay. There is resentment at what whites regard as a disruption of the sacred activities of their sanctuaries, a defiling intrusion upon what they have supposed is their most earnest and innocent effort, their worship. There is dismay because the direct implication of the reparations Manifesto is a challenge to the integrity of white worship and an exposé of those who still attend such worship while countenancing the inherited and continuing alienation of the races in this land and in most of its churches. This black demand, unlike others that have been uttered heretofore, seems to invert everything so far as the white synagogues and churches are concerned. Up to now white religion might have been questioned for doing too little and for doing that too late, for an insufficient generosity, for a resilient apathy, for tardiness, for a condescending spirit, but never before in an effective way have the very presuppositions of white religion in America been contested so that what has been assumed to be holy is seen as unsanctified, or so that shrines can with justification be violated and so that white guilt—accumulative, inherited, corporate guilt—is at last dramatized as the central racial issue in the nation and, particularly, in white religion.

It is a pity that so many whites take umbrage in these circumstances, since the reparations Manifesto embodies the first proposal anywhere advanced in the contemporary days of the American racial crisis, which holds promise of being, at once, legally precedented, psychologically realistic, theologically sound, and viable so far as practical implementation is concerned. It cannot be faulted in American jurisprudence; it confronts the otherwise traumatic and paralyzing reality of white guilt with some imagination and some grace; it has venerable sanction in both biblical faiths; it is capable of being done and done now.

This does not mean that the original scheme, set forth in April 1969 at the Detroit Conference and subsequently brought into some white congregations and presented to some white ecclesiastical councils and assemblies, is or should be immune from criticism. It does mean, to my mind, that the relevant criticism of the Black Manifesto must be directed to its modesty, to its indefiniteness, and to the tentativeness with which it has been advanced, rather than to its substance or to its fundamental rationalization, either legally or theologically.

The Legitimacy of Reparations for American Blacks

Though the publicity attendant to the promulgation of the reparations Manifesto and to the early presentations of it in white sanctuaries has tagged this as a radical or militant move, the truth is that reparations is such an old, established, and much utilized remedy in the law that its invocation in the name of American blacks must be counted as a conservative

tactic and one which, if anything, is long overdue. In ordinary
commerce, for example, reparations are the essential element
of compensatory damages; in the relations of nations in the
aftermath of war, reparations are a traditional resort. Reparations are a *limited* remedy, it must be remembered, appropriate where some harm or injury or wrongful loss has been
suffered for which restitution monetarily can to some extent
restore the party wronged to his position prior to the injury or
other loss. Legally, reparations are to be distinguished from
punitive damages which—in addition to any attempt at restitution—impose costs upon the culpable party as a penalty or
punishment. The conservative posture of the Black Manifesto
is proved at just this point. From three and a half centuries
of chattel slavery, segregation and systematic exploitation, a
simply overwhelming case can be argued for exacting punishment against American whites, but the Manifesto does not
speak punitively and adheres to the idea of reparations, where
some measurable basis for damages, some element of compensation, is controlling.

Reparations represent a limited remedy not only in the
sense that they do not enter the punitive realm, with its inherent imprecision and other ambiguities, but also because a
wronged person or party can never be literally restored to his
former circumstances. Property can be returned, lost or less-
ened income can be computed and paid, physical repairs can
be executed, replacements can be obtained for missing or
broken goods, compensation can be calculated for coercion,
cheating, misrepresentation, lost time and all sorts of other
wrongs, but the practical reparations—the money paid in restitution—can never undo the suffering of the harm as such.
Still, within such limits reparations have proved to be a sen-
sible remedy, and certainly preferable to no remedy at all.

And so it has been considered and utilized in and by this
society not only in the contractual and other business affairs
among and between corporations and persons but also by the
national and other echelons of government. Falsely convicted
and imprisoned persons receive reparations as some gesture
from the state to make up for their loss of freedom and in-

come. Whole classes or categories of people have been paid reparations for wrongs visited upon the group, as has occasionally been the case for some of the Indian tribes, and as was notably the precedent in compensation proceedings finally instituted on behalf of Japanese-Americans who had been wrongfully deprived of their freedom and property by internment during the Second World War. Reparations are still being adjudicated and awarded to victims of Nazism, particularly those who were in concentration camps, and the United States has consistently supported this as a propitious if only partial recourse in these circumstances. The precedent of reparations for those who suffered so brutally from Nazism and for some of their heirs may well be construed as the situation most comparable to that of the American blacks.

Suffice it to say, then, that reparations are a venerable, if limited, nonpunitive remedy, often applicable in relations between individuals as well as groups or classes of persons, governments, and corporations. There can really be no rational opposition to reparations for American blacks on grounds of novelty or lack of precedent.

Yet if reparations do not represent a radical measure in American experience, privately or publicly, the remedy does raise two matters of peculiar significance in the relationships of blacks and whites. They are both issues which have been in one fashion or another suppressed in all those previous discussions, proposals and programs about assimilation, brotherhood, integration, and achieving racial peace, including the so-called war on poverty, the black capitalism schemes, the welfare administration, and the various racial charities of the churches and synagogues.

One of those issues is, of course, the inherent recognition in any reparations plan that an injury has been inflicted or a wrong committed by one against another. There has been *no necessary acknowledgement* of responsibility—much less confession of guilt—on the part of white society, or its people, or any of its institutions, including those religious, in any of these racial programs under either governmental or private auspices. There may be some white folks who have confronted their personal and their inherited and corporate guilt, but the presupposition of the organized efforts in, say, the past fifteen years, in the present phase of the racial crisis in America, has been essentially paternalistic, emphasizing the supposedly gratuitous action of the whites assisting the blacks to overcome some liability or disadvantage which inhibits the blacks from being like the whites. In this context the reparations idea has the enormous virtue of treating racial history in this nation realistically and honestly by the unavoidable implication in reparations that there has been culpable conduct on the part of those who pay the damages.

At the same time, in this remedy the utilization and disposition of a reparations award lies wholly within the control and discretion of the injured party. Up to now, virtually all civil rights, antipoverty, and related enterprises undertaken by the governments, the universities, the unions, businesses and industries, the social work bureaucracies, and the churches have vested control over funding and policy in the whites. If the racial crisis seems not to have been mitigated but in truth aggravated, despite such prodigious exertions by white society, it is because of the anomaly of trying to relieve the victims of a system by perpetuating their dependent and subservient role in that system. Reparations would rectify this by vesting control in the blacks. If that condition is not satisfied, all talk of emancipation and equality for American blacks is fraudulent, and all racial programs are consigned to futility, even where whites are informed by the most benign intentions, as they often are in the churches and synagogues. Unhappily, as has already been witnessed, some religious whites have reacted to the Black Manifesto by increasing or accelerating existing budgets for work among blacks and among the poor and in the inner-cities, and some have had temerity enough to bluntly reject any form of effectual control by those who have been wronged for so long. That can only be heard by the blacks as one more insult to their humanity and as one more provocation to insurrection, though I suppose white churchpeople typically suffer such vanity about their own good intentions that they do not comprehend how they thus compound their offense.

Why Should the Churches and Synagogues Pay Reparations?

It is that same obstinate and naive benignity so characteristic and practiced among white churchmen that accounts for how astonished they have been that any demand for reparations would be addressed at all to the churches and synagogues, or, if at all, why such a Manifesto would be delivered first to them. Surely, in the white religious mentality the construction trades or the bankers or the landlords or the Wallacites or the Mafia or anyone else is to blame, or is more to blame, for these racial troubles. The straightforward answer to that is, obviously, that, to a very substantial extent, all of these constitute the constituency of the churches, and there is no reason for the blacks to forego confronting the churches and synagogues just because the whites tend to be schizophrenic about religion, separating it from their other roles and responsibilities in society.

Moreover, the white ecclesiastical institutions in America are and have long been directly implicated in profiteering from slavery, segregation and other forms of white supremacy through the investment and management of their endowments and other holdings in the American economy. The predominant social witness of the churches racially, for generations, has been incarnated in the wealth and property of white religion, and not in the redundant preaching or pronouncement about racial justice. Indeed, such utterances—made in the context of white racism institutionalized in church economics —can only be construed as gratuitous hypocrisy. The wonder of it all is how a people can so deceive themselves; perhaps they only can when the deception is practiced in the name of God.

The churches and synagogues, in a sense, volunteer as the initial targets for reparations because they claim a surrogate vocation in society as custodian of the conscience of the nation. An issue raised with the churches is thus raised symbolically for all institutions and persons in society and, presumably, it is thus raised in the place of the most mature

moral sensitivity, experience and alertness. The congregations
of white religion have no standing to complain when black
reparationists find them the most fitting forums for their
demands, nor can they ignore or categorically refuse the Black
Manifesto without jeopardizing their vocational credibility as
congregations, nor can they, further, protest because blacks
have been wise enough to anticipate that serving their claims
first against the synagogues and churches would place white
religionists in such an excruciating dilemma.

A parallel logic applies in a broader sense to what white
religion has so familiarly preached and taught. Theologically,
reparations is a means of validating repentance. The citation
from *The Book of Common Prayer,* rendered above, puts
succinctly that which is generally the view in both of the
great biblical faiths to which American white religion asserts
connection. It is proper and appropriate for the Black Manifesto to be first of all heard in the white congregations and
assemblies *just because* it is in those places where repentance
has been preached and *just because* it is there where it has
been taught that repentance requires "restitution and satisfaction, according to the uttermost of your powers, for all injuries
and wrongs by you to any other."

Still, the matter goes much deeper. That which is to be re-
pented of, that repentance which reparations would render as
bona fide, while it manifestly includes all sorts of individual
offenses of specific persons and concerns the defaults and
omissions of men no less than their willful acts and words,
apprehends at the same time the cumulative, corporate guilt
to which all American whites are heirs. There is, one observes,
a now almost monolithic rejection among the whites, both
Christians and Jews, of the reality of corporate guilt. The
famous assassinations of recent years have provoked some concern about the matter, but it seems rather swiftly to have
been sublimated, and the outcomes of the investigations and
the judicial proceedings attendant to each of those assassinations have encouraged such sublimation. Whites in either
church or synagogue might wish that there be no such thing
as corporate guilt, but the insight of the Bible is emphatically
contrary. The second chapter of Genesis is radical in its con-

ception of corporate guilt. The doctrine of the Fall is that men are consequentially related to one another in all things throughout all of time, so that each man bears moral responsibility for that which befalls every other man. In the New Testament, one of the cosmic dimensions beheld in the drama of the Crucifixion is the corporate guilt of all mankind throughout the ages (and not the particular guilt of some hapless pharisees or soldiers contemporaneous with the event). And Saint Paul remains zealous to remind us that not one man is innocent of any of the commandments according to the authority of Israel's witness.

White religionists of all varieties on the present scene may clamour, if they wish, about their innocence in the centuries-old brutalization of American blacks, but let not one indulge the notion that there be warrant for such a wish in the Bible. Meanwhile, it does not take a psychiatrist to discern that the denial of inherited, corporate guilt is a symptom of it. That, of course, points further still to the fact that corporate guilt is a pathological state, a condition of profound disorientation, and even a kind of moral insanity. If that is something of what is concealed and suppressed in the guilt of whites in America, then the reparations idea, requiring as it does a confrontation with the issue of that guilt, is to be heard gratefully by whites, much as an invalid or a diseased man would welcome news that he can be healed.

If reparations represent an apt, if limited, remedy for blacks, and a means of repentance for whites which has veracity for blacks and validity for whites, they also offer an extraordinary opportunity to the white ecclesiastical establishment to be saved from the importunities of other institutions, especially the state. The last years have seen two developments which are ominous so far as the prospect for the churches retaining some freedom and integrity vis-à-vis the state is concerned. One is the accelerating depletion of the human constituency of the great denominations. This trend, occasioned by deaths, dropouts and the refusal of the young to affiliate with institutional religion, coincides lamentably with burgeoning totalitarian tendencies in the state, both in the national government and in the governments of many localities, notably in the great

urban jurisdictions. The transformation of the local police from
civilian to military functions, the assault upon the independence of the courts, the increasing surveillance of citizens, the
instigation of political prosecutions, the preparations for "pre-
ventive detention," the Pentagon's primary initiative in sup-
pressing black protest and quashing other dissent—are but
some few specific evidences of the emergent American totali-
tarianism. On such a scene the great, white ecclesiastical institutions are to be found with a dwindling and ineffectual constituency but at the same time with a staggering wealth fully
capable of maintaining the ecclesiastical fabric even though
the pews are depleted. Such churches, I suggest, become
anxious about their role and influence in society and become
utterly vulnerable to manipulation by other institutions and,
most perilously at this moment, by the state. Analogically, the
white ecclesiastical establishment in America is becoming as
defenseless against the state as the Dutch Reformed Church
is in South Africa, or as pliable as most of the churches became in Nazi Germany. It is the wealth of the American white
churches which is decisive (though not exclusive) in their
vulnerability, and in this light the reparations Manifesto unwittingly, I suppose, affords these churches an opportunity
(perchance a final one) to free themselves as institutions by
divesting themselves of the burden of their wealth.

A Need to Strengthen the Reparations Proposal

Since the promulgation of the Black Manifesto at the Detroit
Conference in the Spring of 1969, reparations as a partial
remedy for the wrongs American blacks have so long and so
ubiquitously endured has received some elaboration. Yet, for
all its strengths in legal principle, in theological rationale, and
psychologically, serious weaknesses of a practical sort exist
in the scheme, and they inevitably invite rejection of the
whole idea of reparations for irrelevant reasons rather than
on the merits. No doubt there is a certain facetious influence
in issuing the Manifesto at all—that is to say, the blacks who
have offered it could be fairly confident beforehand that it

would be scorned by most whites and opposed by any blacks
who have acquired status quo vested interests in the churches
and in society generally. That it would predictably not be
received seriously as a proposal to be implemented by both
races, by some blacks and most whites, but heard instead as
some kind of impertinent gesture may explain the weaknesses
of the original Manifesto considered on the level of practical-
ity, but that is no argument against the amendment and ex-
pansion of the proposal.

I suppose there is a sense in which it is impossible to com-
pute monetary damages for American blacks. The wrongs have
been too many to even fully recall, and they have happened
over nearly four hundred years and the claims and causes of
so many persons are included both in their own names and as
heirs or as other derivative parties. But that is the situation,
with greater or lesser extent, in every reparations case: this
is a *limited* remedy in which what can be done, not what
should be done in perfect equity, is done. By that test, however, the Detroit version of the reparations demand is woe-
fully inadequate in naming 500 million dollars as payment
from the churches. The Manifesto says that blacks will no
longer suffer a few crumbs at the hands of whites, and then
it demands no more than a few crumbs. And that is the case
whether one is concerned with the enormity of the harm or
with the magnitude of the capability of the white churches
and synagogues to pay damages. Regarded from either of
these factors, the $500 million is so nominal an amount as to
refute the essential concept of reparations. More, much, much,
much more must be projected before the reparations Manifesto can be accounted viable.

The white religious institutions which have so far seemed
most receptive to the demand, with only an exception where
sums have in fact been paid, have charged that the National
Black Economic Development Conference, which has volunteered to receive and utilize the reparations, is unrepresenta-
tive of what the whites call "the mainstream" of the American
black community, and have accused the conference of being
too indefinite about how any monies paid would be utilized.
It has been earlier emphasized that in reparations control of

the utilization of payments lies exclusively with the injured claimant, and for the party who has committed the wrong to exercise such control is a contradiction and in the instance of payments by the white churches it would be a preposterous extension of the very paternalism of those churches which is a prominent feature of the harm they have done to blacks.

Moreover, on the issue of who or what can act representatively and responsibly in the black community to receive and administer reparations, the fact is that white supremacy has so inhibited, harassed, and subverted indigenous black community organization that there is no single, unambiguous, ideal black group or institution about which similar complaint could not be made. At that point the conference at least has the credentials which stem from propounding the reparations scheme and acting upon it. In any event, the constitution of a black reparations agency is a problem which blacks alone must resolve.

The twin issues of the composition of such an agency and the administration of reparations might well be clarified if the Manifesto were elaborated in two ways, both of which would also help to bring realism to the matter of the amounts to be paid. One of those would be provision for the filing and adjudication of individual claims, specifying particular acts, events or circumstances in which a person has been hurt in a manner entitling him to reparations. These are the cases in which torts and crimes and civil offenses have been committed against blacks, often casually, by white persons and white institutions, including, to begin with, the clergy and laity of the congregations and the churches, synagogues and ecclesiastical bureaucracies as such. Let whites who complain that the Detroit proposal is too vague be cautioned hereby that if individual claims are made, they may find themselves preferring the vagueness of the Manifesto they now reject.

There is ample precedent for an individual claims procedure in the reparations history of both the Japanese-Americans and the Nazi victims, but the peculiar situation of American blacks may warrant a further means of community reparations whereby in a particular city or town or other region a black community organization is established specifically to prosecute a reparations claim for wrongs which that black community as a whole has suffered or now suffers from whites and their churches and other institutions in the same locality. Such community reparations procedures might vary a good deal in their organization from place to place without the necessity of any single, uniform, national body for oversight or accounting, though that does not obviate or displace the function of the National Black Economic Development Conference.

Some whites will be apprehensive about the elaboration of the reparations proposal by admission of individual claims or those of particular black communities, fearing that Pandora's box would thus be opened. So be it. It is that lid which must be lifted if there is ever to be in this land a confrontation between blacks and whites which is honest, which esteems justice, and which furnishes any prospect of reconciliation one day.

And some white churchmen will assert that such procedures instituted for reparations payable by and through the white synagogues and churches will disclose wrongs for which they should not bear blame and that if there are to be any reparations, other institutions in society besides the churches should be summoned, that perhaps there should be some duly constituted public body—a reparations court or referee or commission—to hear and adjudicate all claims. Perhaps so. The plain truth is that there is now no legislature in the country, including the Congress, practically capable of taking the latter action, though dealing honestly with reparations in the precincts of the ecclesiastical establishment could be a demonstration of what the legislatures should undertake. And if claims received by the churches might just as fairly or even more fairly be lodged against other white institutions, then that does not dismiss the same demand against white religion, given the pervasive role of white religion as an accomplice, where it is not indeed the principal, in American racism.

The Black Manifesto needs, in my view, strengthening and extending in the ways here suggested, or in others, so that it has the solemnity which the principle of reparations in human affairs requires for those who are wronged and for those who have wronged. In that process let it be remembered that the underlying issue is reconciliation, and the categorical necessity of repentance in reconciliation. The chief obstacle now to an effectual reparations program is that white Christians and Jews loathe repentance: they are deceived into supposing they have nothing to repent of, or they are afraid they may repent too much.

There are none who have nothing to repent of, not even one. And it is just as impossible to repent too much as it is not possible to forgive too much.

TOWARD MAKING "BLACK POWER"
REAL POWER

by ROBERT S. BROWNE*

TWICE A YEAR the American Assembly of Columbia University,
an adult education group, holds conferences on topics considered of current interest. The assembly chose to have a conference the weekend of April 26 at Arden House, Harriman,
New York, on black economic development; and, lo and be-
hold, the black community had also organized a conference
with exactly the same title at the same time in Detroit. I was
one of two or three people who attended both; Thursday at
the opening of the Arden House meeting, Friday and Saturday in Detroit, and Sunday morning back for the American
assembly. Unfortunately, I had to catch the last plane out of
Detroit halfway through Jim Forman's talk.

The contrast between the two conferences is very illumi-
nating. They were not precisely the same sort of gathering
even in their intent. The conference in Detroit was attended
exclusively by blacks. It was large. Attendance at Arden House
was by invitation only and was small, about seventy people
roughly divided equally between blacks and whites. The
whites were from the fields of education and business, essentially: several large newspaper publishers, a bank president
and even a Mississippi plantation owner—a nice guy, not like
the image one would have. On the black side, most were businessmen or people who in one way or the other are connected
to the business world, their own business, or working for large

* This chapter is derived from two talks given by Professor Browne.

white firms. There were a few black people from education, and several from social agencies working on the general problem of the ghetto.

The backgrounds of people attending the Detroit conference were far more heterogeneous than those at Arden House, except for the fact that they were all back, which made them homogeneous in that sense. But backgrounds were heterogeneous; very, very poor people from the South and from urban ghettos, black educators and black businessmen, and all walks of life along the spectrum. We had a good cross section of black people at Detroit.

Naturally, neither meeting would have been called apart from the critical period in which black people in America now find ourselves; relatively impoverished in the richest nation the world has known, relatively powerless in a nation which boasts of its democratic processes. In a nation which worships education as the magic key to success, our children go unlettered. In an era of global nationalism, we are people without a nation. Something more than disadvantagement, however, is found in the situation, for the oppression could have been and was cited with validity by Frederick Douglass, Booker T. Washington and W. E. B. Dubois before the 20th century began. The difference is qualitative, deriving from the mood in which blacks, especially the younger ones, are replacing the old passivity and dependency psychology with a psychology of independent action, swapping old gradualism for a new urgency.

Both conferences, Detroit and Harriman, were useful, but their natures were quite different in spite of the common topic of black economic development. Since they were obviously trying to do different things, they are hard to compare. What I think is significant to see is that at the Detroit sessions, I found no feeling that black development can be discussed within a restrictive scope. The Arden House group made an effort to consider specific steps for developing the black community in an economic way. In general we discussed raising the income of blacks and the standards of living of the black community. These two things were the set focuses. So for two and a half days we talked, and specific proposals did come out of that conference.

The Detroit all-black conference, on the other hand, never entertained the idea that a black economic development discussion could constrict itself to such a narrow range. From the first the tone was that we were going to talk about political matters, ideology, capitalism, socialism, integration and all sorts of other things. The Arden House meeting felt these issues would be too controversial and thus concentrated on the narrow concepts of how to raise incomes.

Some of the brothers at Detroit had done ground-breaking work aimed at national black sovereignty, toward a self-governing community taxing itself, conducting foreign relations and trade and legislating law enforcement, property rights, a monetary unit and controls of immigration and emigration. Yet we blacks do not have sovereignty over ourselves as individuals or as a community and are far from nationhood. The conference in April, it seems to me, was for probing for the most promising techniques which can be utilized to maximize black well-being, but it was not interested in bandaids. In contrast to the restricted concerns at Arden House, Detroit centered more on increasing the power of the black community as a necessary precondition for talk about raising incomes. This is probably valid. Essentially, the ills under which black people suffer in the United States result from their having no handles on the basic levers or sources of power.

Missing Levers of Wealth

Incomes can be raised arbitrarily by doubling welfare payments and setting minimums under which big doles are made. A very simple way to raise incomes is by giving people money. As Robert Kennedy once said, "The thing wrong with poor people is that they need money." This is true, although I do not think the message of the Detroit conference was that blacks are interested in having incomes raised that way. They want no handouts. They want to refashion the society in such a way that they will have the incomes both April conferences felt them entitled to have, not by handout method but by developing a society where an equitable income would accrue through the normal course of fate. To accomplish this, the black gathering felt we have to make some basic changes in the society, because now it will not permit black incomes to rise to a level of equality with white incomes. And still nothing is said about the wealth question.

Two separate concepts are involved in the terms "income" and "wealth." One is raising the amounts received annually; the income concept—a flow concept. Related to but nevertheless distinct from income is the concept of wealth—stocked assets. True, the stocked assets an individual, group or society has is a great determinant of income. A significant portion of the incomes in this country are not earned but accrue automatically to those individuals who happen to have great wealth, a lever of power blacks do not enjoy. Black economic development to black people, therefore, means not only increasing the flow received periodically but also getting a share of the stock of wealth. Blacks feel neglected on both scores. Income always gets the emphasis.

Statistics constantly point out that the black income median is so much below the white. Less attention is paid to how much wealth is owned by blacks as compared to how much whites own in the country. The reasons for the disparity, of course, are clear and need not be belabored here. One main reason can be summarized practically. When this nation was being developed—carved up and raped—blacks were a major item of wealth as slaves. We were a form of wealth. Historically, this attitude toward blacks has been carried down. When the country was being divided up, the society did not permit us to be on the receiving end. Mr. Astor's ancestors happened to get the piece of property now called Times Square for a song and, by doing nothing, his heirs a few hundred years later are fabulously wealthy. Blacks could never participate in that kind of thing. The country was parceled out before we were legal individuals; and to the extent that anything was left—and a good deal was—in 1863 when the Emancipation Proclamation was signed, we were still excluded. All the rumors of forty acres and a mule came to nothing. The country was divided, and little titles were drawn up and given to lots of people for whatever reason, but we had no opportunity to take part in the process.

The facts of American history effectively preclude blacks from being among the 153 wealthiest American families which, according to *Fortune* magazine, each have assets in excess of $100 million and which, together with the 200 largest corporations, virtually run the country's economy. It was *Fortune*, not the National Black Economic Development Conference, which listed those who control most of the wealth. Of the 153, not all trace their wealth to the initial division of the national territory, but many of the fortunes were accumulated prior to 1900. The same factors which kept blacks out of the "first families" have prohibited participation in more recent sources of collecting wealth, such as oil. We started too late and had too many handicaps against us when the game began.

Or look at the corporations. *Fortune* listed the 500 largest, but perhaps some 200 wield the major power. Annual incomes of most of those 200 far exceed the budgets of most African nations. The annual revenues of the General Motors Corporation are larger than the gross national product of all but the top 15 nations of the world. Tied in to corporation wealth is the "military-industrial complex" centered in the Pentagon's dealing with the two major corporations. Blacks have no power in this complex. The two or three black generals which we have are not involved in shelling out the taxpayers' money. Nor are blacks at top levels in the corporations, although some may have a black vice-president to deal with black affairs and to see that enough blacks are hired to prevent the firm's being in violation of fair employment laws. I suspect that black vice-presidents have little power beyond such matters.

Missing Levers of Political Power

Another set of power levers on which blacks have no hold relate to government. In the federal administration, blacks have virtually no power at all, although we did get a black man as Secretary of Housing in the Johnson Administration. Admitting that some administrations have articulated considerable sympathy for black problems, I doubt that blacks have much say in the executive branch in Washington. Getting sympathy is hardly the same as having power. If we shift our focus to the federal legislature—much more important than the administration in many instances—we find we have a single senator. One out of a hundred! And nine black U.S. Representatives, out of 435! (That is, a black population of 12 or 13 percent is represented in the House by 2 percent black congressmen.)

The nine representatives is a recent high, and the one who was the most powerful (Adam Clayton Powell) was stripped of his seniority and his committee chairmanship. The Supreme Court, to its everlasting glory, has redeemed him somewhat by reseating him. But it is not just having a vote in Washington that wields power; it is chairing a powerful committee that counts. Even most whites are unfortunate in that respect, because of who runs the powerful committees; Mendel Rivers, John Eastland, these sort of people, who are not only white, but who are reactionary bigots whom many whites think represent them rather badly. They surely do not represent blacks. Rather they are openly antagonistic to our interests—"anti-representation," one might say.

Powerful congressional committees, along with the military-industrial complex, the White House, the 153 families and the corporations run the country. Blacks have no finger hold on any one of these levers of power. (I am leaving out another major power—the Mafia, an organization about which I really know nothing despite *Time* magazine's suggestion that I do. It is my impression, however, that blacks have no leverage in the Mafia either.)

A lack of access to the instruments of power, supplemented by white America's vicious racial prejudice toward blacks, has led to our perpetual impoverishment, our self-hatred and psychological insecurity, our poor educational attainment and our social disorganizations. So blacks are very much concerned now about how to acquire some power, not just how to raise incomes from an average of $4,500 a year to $6,500, although that is important to a man whose income is only $2,000. More income is certainly not to be minimized. Blacks thinking in a larger context, however, are saying we will always be vulnerable to handouts unless we can acquire some control and voice in the nation's power centers.

James Forman and the Black Manifesto, which came out of the Detroit Black Economic Development Conference, have brought attention to the vast sums of money that the churches have. With money comes power. I am not suggesting that the churches wield power to the same degree as the federal administration, the Congress, the 200 major corporations, the 153 wealthiest families or the Mafia. Churches are second rank power-wielders, along with labor unions; powerful, but not the pinnacles of power.

Approaches to Black Economic Development

The Detroit conference, I think, was attempting to wrestle with the issue of how blacks can get a grasp on the levers of power, even secondary levels of power. Rather than recap the story of the Black Manifesto's confrontation with the keepers of the churches' power, I will, in an oversimplified analysis, suggest four approaches to the question of black economic development. Perhaps my analysis consists of only two approaches, reformist and structuralist, each subdivided.

A reformist would say, "society isn't so bad; we just have to make some minor changes." Opposed to this is the structuralist point of view which would say that fundamental changes must be made in the society, not marginal changes which merely put a little more bread on tables or ease pain and suffering. To the structuralist these are minor changes which do not come to grips with the problem.

Take the reformist and structuralist approaches and divide both along the ideological lines of integrationist and separatist; thus, there are reformists who are integrationists and reformists who are separatists, and structuralists who are integrationists and structuralists who are separatists. Admittedly, every independent group cannot be neatly fitted into this pattern, but as a descriptive mechanism these four pigeonholes have value.

Reformist-integrationist: The reformist-integrationist approach is the one on which greatest effort has been put in the past. A reformist-integrationist viewpoint would list the things needing to be done for black economic development in the following order of priority. First, maintain a high level of aggregate demand in the economy; be sure the economy remains prosperous because the number one thing is raising black incomes and standards of living and blacks always fare better in times of prosperity than in depression.

Second priority would be removal of barriers to black employment in all jobs; third would be to get unemployment levels down to white percentages; fourth would be housing. Fifth would be guaranteed annual income, definitely a simple, quick way to raise incomes but one with many drawbacks. I would like to think it would not have too high a priority. Finally, I suspect the reformist-integrationist approach would have to deal with the rural to urban migration problem. It is difficult to work on employment and housing in urban areas if there is constant inundation by new waves of people. Fast running just to stay where you are, an Alice in Wonderland expression, would be needed. To end the migration there needs to be some concerted effort, some economic development effort in the rural communities. Unfortunately, our meagre wisdom about how to effect economic development in urban areas seems well ahead of what we know about development in the rural scene. Since society cannot tackle both scenes with simultaneous effectiveness, the urban problems have the priority. The reformist-integrationist would institute a holding action in rural regions while attempts are made to figure out what to do there.

By a holding action, the reformist-integrationist approach means giving the rural poor, on a permanent basis, money or some equivalent—and giving it where they are but on a nationally standardized base. This would be an alternative to enticing them to go to large cities, like New York, where the system pays them a larger stipend than they get, say, in Mississippi. People would get a low mark in economics indeed if they stayed in Mississippi with a tiny income rather than go to

New York where they can get a large one, not really large, but larger at least than in Mississippi. What the reformist would do is to provide the larger income in rural Mississippi in order to buy time to solve the urban situation.

Reformist-separatist: The reformist via separation would not have many economic points of disagreement with the first approach. The separatist, however, would label the reformist-integrationist too idealistic, saying there is little evidence that society will accomplish very many of the priorities. The second reformist ideology places emphasis on work with black people where they are, in the ghettos. It says the people will not find jobs outside the ghetto, so bring jobs to the ghettos.

Reformist-integrationists would want houses for blacks spread around, while the reformist-separatist would place the new housing in the ghettos. Ideology is an important ingredient contrasting the two. It asks if one foresees a fully integrated American or some separatist arrangement. The reformist-separatist would not want efforts and emotions dictated by that question because the integrated society is so far in the future that no one alive today will see it. He wants to deal with the existing situation, making the ghetto a more liveable place rather than destroy it.

Personally, I feel that the separatists are on the sounder ground on this issue. I see little chance for a fully integrated American society in my lifetime or even in my children's lifetime. It is a disservice to the people living in ghettos for others to say, "No, we mustn't pour money into the ghetto because we'll perpetuate it. We should disperse the ghetto." I think this sacrifices the lives of ghetto people since ghettos are not going to be dispersed in any immediate future. A viable policy is to develop or rebuild the place where the people are.

The argument is classic and is found in many guises. We had a form of it over the separate-but-equal higher education facilities in the South a quarter-century ago. One point of view was that blacks should not accept the separate facilities. I remember particularly the case of Texas State University, a large black school, where, when a court ruled blacks could not go to the University of Texas Law School, the state had to provide a separate facility equal to the white one. Many blacks said, "No, we shouldn't accept a black law school because it just makes it more difficult for us to get into the white schools." The opposing view said, "Yes, but we can't sacrifice another generation waiting until blacks get into white schools. We need some black lawyers now, so let's accept the black law school." In different forms the same argument goes on today, and reasonable men can disagree on which is the correct approach. I feel it is more realistic to say society will be segregated, as far as we can see, and then work from there.

Structuralist, integrationist and separatist: One of the most interesting structuralist arguments I have seen was in an article in the March-April, 1969, issue of the *Harvard Business Review*, "What Do You People Want? Transfer of Big Companies to Black Control," written by Richard F. America, Jr., a black man at the Stanford Research Institute. He says that what is required is for the government to be prepared to spend large sums to transfer at least one major corporation in every industrial category to black control. It could take billions. America wrote that his is the first step toward any economic parity for blacks. That is, until blacks have a steel plant, or control of a steel plant, a fertilizer plant, an automobile plant —the whole range—then we cannot speak of blacks really being *in* the society. Therefore, the *Harvard Business Review* article proposed a massive transfer of wealth.

This is a structuralist change. To a far-out person perhaps the only structural change possible is destruction and replacement of the existing government and capitalist system. The idea out of Stanford might be too mild to the far-out. Most Americans, however, would find it wildly structural, wildly revolutionary to talk of arbitrarily transferring major corporations to black hands. In justification of the proposal, I think a beautiful word has been chosen—*reparations*. I have never understood the furor over this word since it has been used by other groups for years. Maybe it is shocking to some. For reparations! Why else transfer corporations to blacks? The present owners would be compensated out of general government revenue from taxpayers. I think it reasonable. I am amazed the *Harvard Business Review* printed the article, but then the *Harvard Educational Review* printed a very ugly piece about blacks a few months earlier and, no doubt, Harvard prides itself on objectivity.

I would also put Jim Forman's Detroit speech and the demands of the Black Manifesto in the structuralist-integrationist category. The Introduction to the Manifesto definitely suggests some structural changes in the society. The specific projects outlined in the Black Manifesto, not the Introduction but the Manifesto itself, would cause no structural changes. But they are an opening toward change, taking it slowly at first since the public is not really prepared to see what needs to be done and must therefore be allowed to warm up. A few of us used the word "withdrawal" in relation to the Vietnam war as early as 1965, yet it took four years for it to become a respectable term. It may equally take some years for "reparations" (when used by blacks) to become a respectable word to average American ears.

At any rate, I am saying that the Black Manifesto is not directed at structural change itself but seems to be moving in the direction of dealing realistically with basic alterations in power relationships. How is it moving toward structural change? I must go to the fourth approach, the structuralist-separatist, before considering this question.

Forman seems to fit in the structuralist-integrationist slot because there is no hint of separation in his Introduction to the Manifesto. He proposes a program to be done in coalition with whites, albeit with black leadership. The Manifesto itself has been attacked by parts of the black community as putting forth a mere reformist program. Leaders of the Republic of New Africa, for example, have said the National Black Economic Development Conference's call for reparations from the churches is counterrevolutionary. Other parts of the black community say the Black Manifesto (the implementation portion) offers only another reform of an existing system while what is needed is a basic alteration of the system. Some revolutionary language appears in Forman's Introduction to the Manifesto, but the Manifesto itself—its programs and proposals—read reformist and turn off some militant blacks. Also, Forman's Introduction does not take a clear separatist line.

Supporters of The Republic of New Africa, a structuralist/ separatist organization, take the stance that black society *is* a separate society and what we must do is to formalize the separation. The claim is that most blacks live in a separate society from whites so why not regroup the two in their own geographic areas and make it total, giving blacks control over their own lives. The idea is growing in popularity. It is thoroughly structuralist, not necessarily in an economic sense but in a political one. It envisions major change in political America. Severing several states for a new black nation is decidedly a structuralist concept. Not surprisingly then, those who support such action think that what the Black Manifesto is advocating is not structuralist change but reformation, and integrationist-reformist at that. Which are the Manifesto's proposals, reformist or structuralist?

I have agreed already that the programs are basically reforms. I am nevertheless going to put them in the structuralist category because it strikes me that the projects which the Manifesto proposes were chosen neither for their potential profit possibilities nor for any reformist amelioration—most of them anyway. (Certainly the welfare rights business is reformist, as the strike fund may be.) The major ingredients of the Manifesto—the land bank, the television stations, the publishing houses, black universities—are tools for a cultural revolution in black thinking.

Moneymaking endeavors most of them are not, though television stations generally make a profit, I guess. Publishing houses often do not. Universities are not moneymaking, at least that is my impression. The Manifesto proposals, if implemented, could provide the means for educating the public toward the kind of structural changes which I am convinced the Detroit conference felt were necessary before America can be made a liveable place for blacks. Having made ourselves understood, we can then move in the direction of an ideal society, whether it be separate or integrated, which is not so important as blacks getting genuine control of and power over our lives.

No More Illusions of Power

The illusions of power, such as another black in the federal administration's cabinet, are insufficient. Only real power is being sought. I feel the Manifesto's demands are structuralist not because they bring power but because they would educate black people to the need for the quantitative jump toward power. Forty thousand dollars for killing rats in a ghetto is a bandaid; yet I will hardly laugh at $40,000 for such a purpose. It is indeed reformist. But for a parent whose baby is being bitten by rats it is most important. I do not buy the idea that accepting money for rat control is counterrevolutionary. How could it be counterrevolutionary if a mother's child is in danger? Rats must be killed, but the mother who gets rat control must be told not to be excessively grateful, not to feel that the extermination is a great gift. She should be made to understand that much greater things must be done if we are to have a satisfactory society, and that is what the Black Manifesto demands are trying to push toward and why I find them important.

Blacks in America have no bootstraps to pull ourselves up by. We start with so few economic resources that our tactics must be to utilize cleverly what strength we have, namely, the political force of 25 million potentially united black minds, using them to extract some economic resources from those who do have them. In many cases, of course, the resources morally belong to us. Obtaining control of them is not easy and it takes a commitment prior even to the political one, for I have referred to our political force as based on 25 million *potentially united* black minds. Achieving a substantial degree of unity is an obvious prerequisite for rendering the political force effective as a lever for extracting resources.

The Black Manifesto demands are a step toward that unity and political effectiveness. Religious groups have been given the opportunity to fund the first step in the black people's liberation process.

A NONVIOLENT ENDORSEMENT

by JAMES LAWSON

HOW ARE WE to measure the impact of the Black Manifesto and place it in a perspective which can compel an adequate response? The churches dare not simply run away, as some are now doing.* Nor must they simply swallow the Manifesto

* Disagreement with a person's viewpoint and then dismissal of the meaning of the person's work and life influenced, for example, the manner in which both black and white churchmen disagreed with the late Martin Luther King's nonviolence and abjectly failed to evaluate the sacrifice of his life and the meaning of his ministry. Let us disagree with the Manifesto's ideology if we will, but let us not be blind men who fail to see its central thrust upon our times.

I for one seriously differ with those who assert their rights "by any means including the use of force and the power of the gun." "By any means" is the basic ethical view of America. Our official national policy in Vietnam has been and is "by any means." Both the Pentagon and our presidents have used that phrase to justify napalm, escalation and destruction of crops and homes. Western man has rarely been concerned about the way he attains his goals. The ends have justified the means. That is precisely what is behind the doublethink language today: "War makes peace, safeguards society, etc." Any serious revolution today must also overthrow the ethical bankruptcy which makes possible so much cruelty.

Furthermore, racism, violence and poverty are demonic powers. They are interlocking cruelty systems on the American scene. "By any means" plays into their hands. "By any means" makes no encounter with them. On the contrary, "by any means" enables the nation to move towards her own latent final solution—a racist Fascist state which will make Hitler look like a Sunday school trouble-maker.

This issue requires far more examination than black people are giving without regard to their calling, an error, however, to be preferred to what is generally occurring. Through this event believers must sense the direction of God and exert ourselves in cooperation.

The Black Manifesto is one more element in the onrushing, worldwide social revolution which today embraces every people, every nation, every race and continent, every ideology and faith. We must stop being afraid of revolution. Social revolution simply does not inevitably mean violence. It means that rapid social change is the first trait of history today. World upheaval affects persons with the demand for newness, confounds old ideologies, and threatens outmoded institutional patterns.

Violence often accompanies social revolution, but far more frequently, it marks the use of power by the decision makers to preserve the status quo, or to control the revolution or to deflect it to an alternative course.

Two illustrations may clarify this point. The industrial revolution shaped the 20th century more than any of the wars of this century. The expanding chasm between the "have" nations and the "have not" nations comes primarily from the appetite of the factories of the West for raw materials, cheap labor and markets. Responsible international controls even fifty years ago would have preserved a stable world.

Many young people romanticize the Cuban Revolution. However, Castro used violent force primarily to overthrow Batista, to seize power and to reorganize the land. Now the real revolution in Cuba goes on as Castro leads the people to new ideologies as he experiments with new educational, social, political and industrial institutions.

Three drives impel and provoke social change in a variety of forms but always toward the fulfillment of three objectives.

The first objective concerns the worth of a human being. What is a man? What does it mean to be genuinely alive? I was in Australia in 1965 speaking to various church and peace groups on my trip to Vietnam. In Sydney at 4:00 A.M. I

---

it. I want black people to be the instrument of a great new ideal for this land. Accepting the ideologies of cultural America without question can prove disastrous.

received a call from an aborigine spokesman who wanted to
visit. We talked while we ate breakfast. I was impressed with
his emphasis upon restoring the dignity of his people, a dignity crippled by the treatment of the whites.

The late Martin Luther King constantly emphasized the
theme of "somebodyness." The Memphis Sanitation Strike of
1968 adopted as a motto, "I am a man." This stress on human
dignity and freedom holds another element of unity. One finds
again and again throughout the world a sense of human
solidarity and kinship. Malcolm X saw this when he made his
journey to Mecca. He discovered the powerful motif of brotherhood, of relationship, of union with mankind. It transformed
his sense of participation in the struggle for a better life.

The second objective of social revolution today is to restore
human life to its proper place of value. This in part explains
the overwhelming impatience with cruelty in any form. Our
young rebels best illustrate this intolerance of cruelty. They
want to stop it now. Rightly or wrongly, the young revolutionaries think that most of us over thirty have too many
excuses. We plead that ending cruelty takes time, and we do
nothing to speed up the process. Perhaps better than most
citizens, students see the extent to which our society has gone
wrong. And they perceive the interlocking system of cruelty:
poverty, violence and racism which caused our society to
deteriorate. The attitude of the young toward the Vietnam
war is an example of their demand for an end to cruelty:
"Stop the war." "Withdraw our troops." "Make love, not war."
"No Viet Cong ever called me nigger." "Hell no, we won't go."

Many of the young merely reflect the overwhelming emphasis on love and peace and hatred of evil in today's social
revolution. They also seem more prophetic than most church
leaders, and they reflect Jeremiah's impatience with evil:

> See, I have set you this day over nations and kingdoms,
> To pluck up and to break down
> To destroy and to overthrow
> To build and to plant.   (1:10)

We may detest the rhetoric and demonstrations which
threaten to burn and destroy. However, we must admit that

far too many of our institutions are the last bastions of cruelty. They destroy, not by burning or looting, but by starving the poor.

Few if any Americans want children to go hungry. Yet children in many of our urban and rural areas *are* hungry. In Memphis we are now daily testing children under six who suffer from hunger and malnutrition. We have now trained about twenty neighborhood aides to walk the streets to find these children. We prescribe the medicine of food. Through the resources and skills of St. Jude's Hospital for Children we attempt to help them recover. Why are children going hungry if only a few of our citizens wish it? Hunger stalks our streets because many of our institutions are blind to human need. Many of our forms of social order produce hunger and poverty. Many of our institutions allow us to operate as though the times were not changing and people were not hurting. Again and again when a group of citizens comes to see the need, the institution stands as a bulwark against their movement to end hunger and malnutrition.

Perhaps Jeremiah and many of the young are entirely correct. Perhaps the old forms must be brought low and their often demonic power broken before new forms can emerge.

The spirit of change now abroad could well show the churches where they fail today. We are floundering for ethical direction. Will we find it in purely academic settings or on Sunday morning at 11:00? No. We may discover genuine directions to the Kingdom of God when we decide that with our bodies and all our resources we will demand the end of cruelty now, and that we will join and support every serious effort to halt inhumanity. Such determination may well produce a more decent earth.

Doctor King often spoke of "the redeemed society." The World Council of Churches coined the phrase, "the responsible society." Those of us who participated in the southern struggle of the last decade rarely spoke of an integrated society. Much more frequently we talked about new cities, freedom cities and a new age. Our general goal has often been termed a "new South." Our nonviolent campaigns always aimed at quite specific and limited goals, such as desegregated lunch counters or bus stations. But we also saw ourselves building a movement that would one day require the reconstruction of the whole land. We did not try to define what that reconstruction represented. Many of us still believe that the new institutions which will emerge must be molded by dignified and free men who have put an end to all the old cruelties.

Let me say again that rapid social change everywhere today clearly demands the rediscovery of genuine personhood, the ending of indecency and the transformation of society. The struggle for racial justice in the United States is the most dynamic and in many ways the most creative western wing of social revolution. I cannot go into great detail here but perhaps a few assertions will provoke the thought necessary to talk about the Black Manifesto.

The struggle for racial justice began in Montgomery, Alabama, on December 5, 1955, where 50,000 black people joined a movement to obtain better treatment on the buses. They engaged in nonviolent, direct action by boycotting the buses. They hurled a challenge at white segregated and racist America. White southerners quickly saw what this meant. Their brothers in other parts of the country did not.

Even fewer Americans saw that those 50,000 black people also challenged and judged Negro civil rights efforts. While Africans and Asians were engaging in direct action, violent and nonviolent, for freedom, Negro churches and civil rights groups were going to court, a method reserved for the middle class and the educated. They were also writing letters of protest, or they were making strong statements of protest. But they were not doing the only thing that brings about real change: organizing black people to act together toward common goals. America needed confrontation, and only a united people had power for direct action. Too often, Negroes expected white people or groups to take the initiative. Leaders of the Montgomery bus boycott insisted that black people must start the action and must make the decisions.

Montgomery, 1955, was as much a judgment upon dormant black people around the nation as upon white racism. It was a challenge to Negro leadership and civil rights groups as well as white institutions. The confrontation process which began in Montgomery produced its own leaders. From this first confrontation Martin Luther King, Jr., Ralph Abernathy and others emerged and became the symbols of the new ideal for America. But the approach which Montgomery ignited was resisted by both black and white across the nation. Despite this resistance, campaign after campaign of confrontation, direct action and aggressive nonviolence rocked the nation. No accounts have given proper consideration to the extensiveness of these efforts or to the goals of the people who organized them. When the churches, that is, the white churches, finally joined in force, they insisted upon a compromising stance which watered down confrontation (the Washington March, 1963).

Another interesting feature of those years is that Negroes generally interpreted the campaigns, not according to the ideologies of Dr. King and others who took the risks and laid their lives on the line. Instead, most Negroes accepted the views of the press. For example, read the definitions of nonviolence by certain black intellectuals who say that nonviolence is passivity or the status quo. You can criticize Martin Luther King, Jr., but you cannot call his life and work passive. You cannot say that he sustained the status quo.

Nonetheless, the nonviolent direct action movement did arouse the nation. Black and white alike awoke to the realities of poverty and racism, and America began its experiments in social change. Martin Luther King, Jr., no matter how we may now dismiss him, is truly the father of "Black Revolution."

The Black Manifesto and the actions taken to support it are evolutionary developments of confrontation but not really radical ones. Many people object to the thesis of reparations. It is too hard a word. Reparations come after wars, and we are not at war. We are not dealing with a defeated and victorious people. We are a single nation. We are not responsible for the sins of our fathers. But let's walk around the theme of reparations.

In the first instance, our nation often gave its citizens opportunities to establish themselves. Take the Homestead Acts of the last century. Any person could move to the frontiers, clear and settle the land, and then the land belonged to him. His toil and risk purchased the land. This chance excluded both slave and free Negroes. In spite of the vision and perception of a few people, no such offer was made to black people after the Civil War.

Look at this idea of reparation in another way. Who cleared the wilderness of the South and built the cities? Who farmed the land? The slaves became the workmen, the carpenters, the blacksmiths, the farmers, the brick masons. They were the technicians who constructed towns and villages. But they were never compensated.

Furthermore, towards the end of the 19th century when as free men they might have received proper wages for their skills, the movements for repression systematically prevented development of their skills. At one time Negroes were the craftsmen. Today the craft unions are the most segregated in the land. Negroes did not volunteer to be unskilled. The nightriders and the KKK used the weapons of tyranny to strip them of their usefulness, and white racist power structures consented. So, rightly, Martin Luther King often spoke of the unpaid check which America owed the Negro.

In Memphis 27.4 percent of the people are poor. This is the second highest rate of poverty in our country. Sixty-six percent of these people are black. Many of them come from the cotton belt. They have less than a fifth grade education. Why? Primarily because the schools for Negroes in this region were developed as control centers for the two seasons that the children were not in the cotton fields. White Boards of Education did not intend to permit black children to become persons of dignity who possessed intellectual and spiritual tools. The products of such a system cannot compete with their peers.

But how can you reverse the cruel consequences of such a deliberate public policy? Black leaders have long called for those massive programs which could reverse the effects of inadequate education. Not too long ago hundreds of black leaders and organizations created the "Freedom Budget." This Budget was submitted to the churches and to Congress. That was that. Nothing was done. Instead, we got the vast outlay of sums for the Vietnam War and for the space program.

The National Urban League has called for a "Domestic Marshall Plan." The Kerner Report and the Urban Coalition insist that only massive programs can end urban unrest, clear slums and give the poor an equal chance.

You do not like the term "reparations." It is too hard a word. Then why haven't the churches or white liberals picked up the cudgels for the predecessors of the Manifesto?

The churches have had since 1955 to establish new priorities and to apply pressures upon government to obtain the legislation that will relieve the masses of the black and poor. If you did not take any of these earlier efforts seriously, why should we now assume that you are genuine in your dismissal of the term "reparations"? Would not black people now be quite naive and foolish if they assumed that your objection to a term is the real issue?

To what extent have the churches urgently sought to rid themselves of their racist past? As one reads the various denominational responses to the Manifesto, one sees bland words filled with emptiness. One such statement reads: "We reject the black racism of the Manifesto. Equally we reject the white racism which pervades American society and in which all of us have shared—sometimes deliberately, most of the time unconsciously, sometimes against our will." Here is one of the favorite cultural tricks. Black racism and white racism receive equal billing. Many white church members have made Martin Luther King and Bull Connors, or the NAACP and the KKK, extremists of equal ill repute. Worse than that, the congregations of the white church which made the above statement are among the most racist in the country. They are strangely quiet except when they periodically cop out in support of law and order.

The Black Manifesto came upon the churches like an "evil from the North," speaking destruction and judgment. Jeremiah did not get hung up on the ideology from the North. He knew that God was perfectly capable of using imperfect vehicles for judgment, yea, even unbelieving instruments. He had a deep awareness of the power of God through events rather than through ideological wrangles. And he was prepared to let God's judgment have sway. Jeremiah believed that the *event* was the word, rather than that the *word* was the event.

Of course, the churches have become so conditioned to cloak the word in *words* that happenings in history through which God wrestles with us leave us unmoved and unchanged. But the Manifesto could not have sparked such hysteria and breast-beating had it not come like a thunderbolt out of nowhere which contained that encountering moment to catch us guilty and defenseless. And that is the simple embarrassing word of the Black Manifesto breaking in upon us through what SCLC called, "a crude, but determined prophet. . . ."

How much more time do the churches need? During the 40's your student groups were calling for integration of the churches. What happened? While the NAACP was brilliantly provoking the Supreme Court to make the Constitution speak for the poor and black, how did you respond? When Bayard Rustin moved with such force in church circles calling for nonviolent action did the churches encourage students and others to organize and begin? On the contrary, in 1950 the churches by and large blessed the Korean War and held the critics in contempt.

When black people in Montgomery appointed Martin Luther King as an articulate spokesman for direct action, did the churches embrace him? How often we heard the cry then from churchmen, "I agree with his goals, but his methods can only cause trouble." What methods did the churches use to tackle the problems long evident? Was not the "methods" excuse simply another way to let God's events pass us by without effecting a meeting?

The churches ought to rejoice in the Black Manifesto. It is a sign of God's grace. He cares about the church. God takes a black leader with a tired ideology, an ideology that is in many parts of the world an enemy of social change, a black leader not really in the center of things, a black leader with open antichurch feelings; and God makes such a black leader a mouthpiece. Then this black leader insists that the church does have power and influence today, that the church is im-

portant for the kind of society we want, that the church can
be an effective instrument for the healing of the races. Should
we not fall on our knees and thank Brother Forman for making us so important? Could he really be wrong?

The Black Manifesto exhorts us to repentance. Simply
stated, the Manifesto asks the churches to turn around and
follow another master. How is this to be done? Here again
we must act instead of mouthing words. Repentance is not a
prayer of confession; repentance is a fresh deed which points
to newness. Repentance is redressing wrongs. The call to
judgment requires repentance. That is our choice. Repentance
demands that we move with haste, even haste that causes
extra mistakes. We must break the chains of the past which
deny the churches the freedom of Christ.

Repentance is the context for understanding the use of the
term, "reparations." Strip the term of its wartime uses. Give
it prophetic use. Placed within the context of repentance,
reparation becomes the specific deed or deeds which confirms
the sincerity and reality of penitence. Through the Manifesto,
God would not have us confess our guilt in nice resolutions
or in prayers of confession. He would have us see that now
is the time for the churches to act with the fruits of new life.

How can reparations from the churches to the program of
the Manifesto reflect genuine repentance? To implement the
programs suggested by the National Black Economic Development Conference (the creation of the Black Manifesto)
requires new priorities and very likely new structures and
missions by the churches. In most respects the programs are
traditionally American (contradicting certain features of the
Manifesto's more radical stance). However, these ventures
could have far-reaching results. The emphasis on communica-
tions obviously seems a way of pulling black people together
in common purposes. It could help to break the hold that
white racist information and news centers have on the poor
and black. We could also give the liberal whites of the nation
centers of information on which they could rely. This could
provide us with workable ways to build meaningful and
powerful coalitions. Subsidized publishing interests (like the
church publishing interests) would not have to think primarily

in terms of profits (at least initially). Instead, they could stress the freeing of people's minds and the liberating of educational institutions.

The churches cannot become a part of such a revolutionary venture without radical repentance. This means a deliberate act of redirecting their financial resources. Let me illustrate this by considering my own denomination, the United Methodist Church.

The national program effort depends on World Service funds which amount to about 25 million a year. All of the boards and agencies (education, evangelism, missions, lay activities, etc.) receive a percentage of these monies, which are apportioned to each annual conference and each local church. We call this World Service, but most of the emphasis remains upon housekeeping chores and very traditional projects. Hence we have a national apparatus which could disappear. It will not disappear because of institutional momentum and self-perpetuation. And World Service funds make this possible. From the point of programming, the national apparatus has not made the local church an effective instrument for real mission. On the contrary, the white congregations still flee from the issues of the city. And the black congregations remain aloof from black revolution, or from feeding that awakening with the stuff of the gospel. Crucial to the awakening is a historical force for redemption rather than another American heresy resulting in chaos and destruction. In other words, the results of the last twenty-five years of World Service in the local church do not warrant United Methodists' insistence upon its present way of handling national efforts.

Therefore, I say, let us do away with this apparatus. We can take the World Service funds and direct them to working in movements for social change and justice. Cut the amounts for housekeeping and for servicing the local churches to a minimum. Rule out the vast numbers of staff and board meetings. Instead, we can develop a number of small urban and rural task forces which can concentrate on the retooling of lay and clergy ministries on ecumenical and conference lines.

The principle of reparations can then be used by God in the United Methodist Church and all other churches as a means to enable us to rediscover ministries and missions. If the church can be transformed from a white middle class, racist American entity, if the church can become a "people of God" enrolled in his kingdom and engaged in costly risk for the kingdom, such an "altogether new thing" can emerge only from an almost irrational (foolishness of God) obedience to the Christ "loose on the world." Transformation cannot come from 475 Riverside Drive or from Nashville. These citadels of United Methodism may in fact be the first hindrances to God and man, the greatest obstacles to mature and Jesus-styled ministries.

Will the apparatus be missed? It's not very likely. Will the church lose ground? The churches already lose ground in the minds and lives of the American people. They are far outside their critical concerns, too far removed from the areas of their disease (or perhaps they are an aspect of our social disease). Their lack of relevance already threatens the present and future of the churches in America. The churches are often the enemies of men; they are barriers to the healing of the races and the nations. If they are not conscious enemies, then they are enemies by default, or worse, by gross distortion of gospel-engendered ministries.

Revamping of churches in this fashion will cause many members to consider withdrawal of their financial support and participation. Already a number of ecclesiastics are deeply harassed by this possibility. The Black Manifesto has indeed conjured up fresh awareness of this threat. This is an overt display of cultural religion. What should we say? For how long will church leaders remain trapped in the cultivation of the tares? Shall we continue to delay the inevitable and postpone radical obedience while we cultivate the weeds in the false hope that somehow the weeds will produce wheat?

At some point those who sincerely wish for the transformation of the churches must brush the dust from their garments and move on to the next task, leaving the people of that village in the hands of God. The hope for them is that God will use the faithfulness of those who obey as a vigorous, visible word, a word which can break through some of the cultural religion and sweep some of these weak men toward faith. In any case, unless the churches risk alienating some of the names on the rolls, transformation and reconciliation will become impossible.

Let it be said as forcibly as possible. My real hope in the effect of the Black Manifesto is not related to the ideology or the specific program which is clearly not dependent upon the introductory discourse. This most recent thrust at the conscience and work of the church can achieve much more than that. I believe that the Manifesto could prove to be another catalytic agent to change the will of the church and the nation.

When we examine racism in our land today, we can begin to see that there are more potential solutions to problems than the American people are ready to adopt. In certain fields, with proper planning and technical information, we could rid ourselves of the cruelty. Proper care of the elderly and the young can be achieved. There is no earthly excuse for hunger in America. We have sufficient resources to eliminate hunger.

But the will of the nation is committed to institutional racism, to policies which produce the Vietnam War and programs which allow poverty to rage without positive opposition. Can the will of the nation be transformed?

I believe it can. And I believe that the churches are a major key.

Church resolutions mean little. But if the nation saw the churches using their own resources and energies for the needs of the poor, the hungry and the black, the churches could become the incarnation for the nation. In other words, churches risking death on behalf of "the least" might become a visible word which would ignite the will of the American people toward social justice.

A final word on reparational relief by the churches. In the Sermon on the Mount, Jesus makes a very pointed judgment on those who are called to the Kingdom of God movement: "If you go to the altar and find that your brother has a grievance against you, leave your gift at the altar. First go and be reconciled to your brother, then come and offer your gift at the altar."

The implication is that those of the kingdom do not have a

grievance against a brother. No follower of Jesus holds grievance against another, even if he is clearly provoked.

Furthermore, the grievance of the brother may be unwar-
ranted. Many churchmen today say that they are not responsible for the way former generations of whites treated blacks.
It doesn't matter. Our brothers have a grievance against us.
The black brother holds a grievance against the white brother.

Jesus asserts that our going to the altar is in vain, that such
worship in a context of the brother's grievance is nothing at
all. What is the white church to do? Under the word of
Christ, your buildings and services are noise that God refuses
to hear. Yes, you might as well be out fishing or golfing.

The white church at the altar has no redemption without
the brother on the outside. We are interdependent. To be the
church of Jesus Christ, the churches must leave their gifts at
the altar and be reconciled.

Here also the black Christian has his calling. Whether we
like it or not, and whether you like it or not, in obedience to
Christ we keep coming to you who have grievances against
us not of our own making. We offer you again and again, by
the very grace of God, reconciliation.

PENANCE:
FROM PIETY TO POLITICS
Reparations as a Religious and Political Issue

by HARVEY G. COX

PANICKY PROTESTANT church opinion to the contrary, James
Forman did not invent the word "reparation." It is a common
idea in legal terminology. It describes the repayment of
money, or other services, that a damaged party receives from
those inflicting injury. The payment of reparations is a long-
standing and accepted procedure of civil law and dates back
to the ancient courts of equity. It is based on the common
moral assumption that a man who is damaged by the actions
of another deserves to be recompensed for that damage.

There can be little doubt that Americans of African extraction have been enormously damaged both by private and
public policy in the United States of America since the arrival
of the first African slaves in 1619. Not only did the institution
of slavery provide for the entrapment, transport, and forced
labor of millions of Africans, but the policy of separating families resulted in untold damage to the culture, social system and
personality structure of the slaves. Even after the abolition of
slavery in the United States, public policies of discrimination
and segregation continued to inflict damage on this group of
people within American society as a whole. The question now
arises: can the damaged party claim reparation from the
society and the state (which represents that society) for damages inflicted? It is my opinion that, until the penitence of
white Americans for the damage inflicted by racism turns

from the area of charity and toward that of concrete reparation, we will remain in our current impasse.

Some people contend that, although individual reparations may be morally justified, there are no precedents whatever for claiming such group reparations and that the idea really has no ethical merit. I believe this is a mistaken opinion. What are the precedents in American history for a program of reparations to black Americans?

The Congress has frequently enacted programs which are of benefit to particular *sections* of the country and only very indirectly to others. We have a history of legislation aiding rural areas, for example. More recently we have the Tennessee Valley Authority and, quite recently, the program for the redevelopment of Appalachia. All of these programs resulted in the flow of Federal funds to an area in need.

But are there examples of federal programs which aided particular *groups* of people without reference to specific geographical area? We all know of subsidies given to farmers, the subsidies provided to the merchant marine and to other special groups within the society. What about groups without a common vocation or occupation?

Here the best example is the G.I. Bill. It is especially important because it bears a certain analogy to reparations for blacks. The G.I. Bill was passed because Americans believed that a whole group of young men and women had been deprived of the normal opportunities of American life through no fault of their own. They had been plucked out of jobs and schools and sent to defend their country. They were thus deprived of the opportunities for education, for home ownership and for developing job tenure. The G.I. Bill provided low interest loans for home ownership, scholarships for education and the assurance that the time away from the job would not count against the accumulation of seniority. Can there be any question that our society has also deprived blacks of home ownership, education, and job opportunities? Can there be any question that this was done without the consent of those damaged by the policy? The parallel here seems obvious.

But are there precedents for repayment to racial or ethnic

groups by the government? It is common knowledge that the Federal Republic of Germany has sought to pay reparations to those Jews who survived the holocaust. In the U.S.A., the American Indian comes immediately to mind. We should all be aware of the enormous damages inflicted on the original Americans by our government's policy of forced relocations, genocide, and deprivation of freedom. The government has tried to make reparations to the Indians, even though these efforts have been sporadic, feeble, and insufficient. Another example is the decision of the government to repay Americans of Japanese ancestry for the financial losses they incurred during their forced relocation into internment camps during World War II. Here again the repayment is ludicrously inadequate. Japanese Americans are able to claim damages up to ten cents on each dollar lost. But even this inadequate repayment is more than anything yet offered to Americans of African ancestry for the damages inflicted on them by relocation, slavery, and official discrimination.

The ethical case for an official government policy of reparations to Afro-Americans is clear. It should consist mainly of cash payments but could also include the other advantages sometimes made available to veterans, such as special job opportunities under civil service.

There are some who have argued that the whole concept of reparations, although it may be ethically justified, is totally lacking in political feasibility. Although at the moment this seems true, it is dangerous to predict what might become politically feasible in the near future. In any case, the churches do not have to wait for *political* feasibility. As beneficiaries of the years of exploitation of black people, they can begin to pay reparations now.

But churchmen must do more than pay as churchmen. They should also work for *public* reparations. White Americans who are committed to justice for all people, who feel the need to express positive and creative penitence for the tragic history of the relationship between the races in our country, have an excellent opportunity. Their penitence can move out of the area of charity and pious pronouncement into the area of politics and structural change. They can work within the existing political structures in their own communities, and in the community at large, to encourage that notion that our whole society has a debt that it *must* pay to black Americans. This debt is not a charitable contribution but an honest debt, and the majority group in America remains the debtor group. Only when the relationships between the two groups are put on this basis of legal right and wrong and of just reparation do we escape the unconscious condescension which so often distorts even the most well-intentioned individual in this delicate area. Only when penitence moves from *piety* to *politics* does it acquire real significance.

PUTTING IT TO THE CHURCHES

by STEPHEN C. ROSE

IN LATE APRIL, more than 500 black militants met in Detroit for the first National Black Economic Development Conference. The three-day meeting was the brainchild of Lucius Walker, the youthful director of the Interreligious Conference for Community Organization, which funded the meeting. It was, said Walker, the first major attempt to link issues of local community organization to the broad question of economic development for millions of blacks who find little help in token programs of black capitalism.

Among the invited speakers at the Detroit meeting was James Forman, International Director of the Student Nonviolent Coordinating Committee, and it was here that Forman chose to gamble on the willingness of the Detroit 500 to be "taken over," the possibility of firing the imagination of uncommitted blacks with a new strategy, and the readiness of the religious establishment to divest itself of some $500 million in what Forman (unfortunately) called "reparations." ("The word reparation is a problem for some," says Lucius Walker. "But our concern is to get funds to where they are needed. Either we get reform bloody quick, or bloody revolution.")

Subsequent publicity has played up Forman's dramatic confrontation at Riverside Church in New York, where on May 4 he read demands from a pulpit vacated by the church's ministers, and the occupation of national Presbyterian offices by supporters of Forman's crusade in a successful effort to wring concessions from the 3.2-million-member Presbyterian denomination. But the story begins with Forman's Manifesto —a highly rhetorical presentation of suggestions put forth at the Detroit conference.

The introduction to the Manifesto is the speech which Forman delivered, entitled, "Total Control as the Only Solution to the Problems of Black People." "Our hearts go out to the Vietnamese," he said, "for we know what it is to suffer under the domination of racist America. Our hearts go out to our brothers in Africa, Santo Domingo, Latin America and Asia who are being tricked by the power structure of the U.S. which is dominating the world today. These ruthless, barbaric men have systematically tried to kill all people and organizations opposed to its imperialism. . . . We must commit ourselves to a society where the total means of production are taken from the hands of rich people and placed in the hands of the state for the welfare of all the people. This is what we mean by total control. And we mean that black people who have suffered the most from exploitation and racism must move to protect their black interest by assuming leadership inside of the United States of everything that exists."

But how? Forman ended by declaring that "we" had the "revolutionary right" to seize power at the Detroit conference based on the program in the Manifesto.

Essentially, the Manifesto of which the Detroit conference approved by a two-to-one margin—but with 100 abstentions— is a general prescription for political and cultural solidarity among blacks and for the beginning of independent economic development along separatist lines. It proposes that the $500 million needed to implement the demands of the Manifesto be raised as reparations from American Christians and Jews. Lucius Walker says that the debate in Detroit was not over the rhetoric of the document ("White Christian churches are . . . used by the government . . . to exploit the people of Latin America. . . . To win our demands we will have to declare war on the white Christian churches and synagogues") but over whether Forman's specific proposals were radical enough—some saw them as "too reformist."

With the formation of the committee and its acceptance of his Manifesto, Forman got over his first hurdle. But how seriously it will ultimately be accepted in the black community at large remains to be seen. The National Committee of Black Clergy issued a supportive statement following the Detroit meeting, but older black leaders have criticized both Forman and the Manifesto for extremist and separatist tendencies. The Rev. Thomas Kilgore, Jr., new president of the American Baptist denomination, suggests that already established funding procedures would have to be brought into play to effect a compromise between Forman's separatism and the political realities of church programming.

Both blacks and whites have been critical of the tactic of disrupting worship. Forman, incidentally, "disrupted" only one service—at Riverside Church—and this was done after prior consultation with the minister, Ernest Campbell, and in a reasonably decorous fashion. Forman sat in the front row with eight companions. He rose, seeking to speak. Thus interrupted, Campbell, his ministerial colleagues and about two-thirds of the 2,000-member congregation departed. Forman had his say, left; Campbell returned, spoke favorably of the concept of reparation while suggesting (along with many church leaders) that the word restitution would be more appropriate. The next day Riverside presented Forman with a restraining order precluding further disruptions; Forman burned the document while attaching his demands to the door of the offices of the Lutheran Church in America. After early May, Forman did not need to use confrontation to achieve a hearing. Forman has been politely received in major assemblies of several Protestant denominations. And in mid-May, an international consultation on racism sponsored by the World Council of Churches issued a statement from London saying: "We urge religious institutions to divest themselves of their excessive material wealth by immediately allocating a significant portion of their total resources, without employing any mechanism of control, to organizations of the racially oppressed." (Though the World Council has never paid reparations, it has channeled funds to various liberation groups in Africa.)

It is still too early to tell what will happen as a result of the Black Manifesto. One can only suggest that the demand is just; the time is right; and a proper response by the white churches would be the painful prelude to something like an appropriate commencement of something new in America.

The nation has never provided adequate recompense to blacks for the years of slavery and degradation. Nor has it been willing to recognize and repair the damage it is still doing to blacks. And it is precisely the missionary task of the church—as a leaven—to do what the society leaves undone, not in order to become a substitute for the government but rather to symbolize the way ahead for the world. Now that reparation is being demanded of the churches, there can be no alternative but positive response. But how, and with what effects? And what if the churches do not respond? Here are a few tentative ideas:

(1) Reparation in the amount demanded clearly would involve the actual transfer of some existing denominational assets from the white churches to the black community; it might be argued that transfer of mission endowments, for example, would be too easy, that the reparation money ought to come from the pockets of the membership. One is tempted to suggest that the reparation be made with deliberate speed both through a massive canvass, where each member, for example, is asked to give $10, and that if the goal is not reached, the balance be provided through transfer of denominational assets.

(2) The request for reparation will raise the question of who will get the money and with what good result, assuming it is forthcoming. From the standpoint of one interested in the renewal of the *white* church, that question is irrelevant. The money asked for, though not inconsiderable, is relatively unimportant in terms of potential social change. Besides it is the *black* community that should, by rights, determine the use of the funds. Perhaps the infusion of $500 million will be the vehicle for creating a certain degree of black unity, or a reshuffling of black leadership, but that cannot be a concern of the white church. In this situation the white church is simply called to make reparation, and the benefits of that act

should be seen not only in terms of the black community but of the white community.

(3) What would the precipitous raising of $500 million mean for the white churches? It could mean the possibility of renewal if reparation is seen as tied to concerns about unity, faith and order. The call for reparation provides a rallying point that is ecumenical, since it is addressed to white churches. More important, ecumenical action of a bold sort would pave the way for valid church union. If we are to have Protestant church union through the Consultation on Church Union (COCU)—the creation of a more progressive church that will also emphasize lay action in the world as the preferable means of social action—then we must conceive of how we might disestablish the vast, relatively autonomous, mission and Christian education establishments of our present denominations.

The call for reparation suggests a novel means of accomplishing this transformation, a means both symbolic and practical. Doubtless the combined assets of COCU denominations, not to mention the assets of white churches within the National Council of Churches, where the plea for reparation was early made, would be more than that requested by the Black Manifesto. Let the white churchmen involve themselves in the process of reparation by calling simply for the raising of the amount demanded.

(4) Assuming there will be pressure from blacks upon the financial enclaves of the white churches, there can also be pressure by whites. We suggest that membership in a direct action campaign to free church assets and money for reparation be opened to individuals who will contribute substantially of their personal resources to the same cause.

(5) If such a process begins, then the denomination can claim honestly to their constituents that they are acting not out of slavish, self-flagellating response to black demands but out of a profound hope in the ingenuity and goodwill of people at the grass roots. The sacrificial move of the denominations would be a signal for the formation of supportive white task forces around the country to carry the reparation issue into each local congregation.

And in the context of this process a provisional commission on church union and faith and order might be established to see how the new life breathed into the church by the act of reparation could be channeled into a restructure of the presently dying ecclesiastical establishment. Reparation is thus neither social stratagem in the service realm or guilt-ridden response; it is, instead, a strategic move with potential implications for faith and order.

(6) If denominations do no more than study the reparation proposal, it is our task to force action. But denominational executives can still lead the way by tendering resignations and recommending that their jobs remain unfilled until the boards and bureaus they have are reconstituted. Such resignations, especially if coordinated and aimed at placing future mission responsibility firmly on lay shoulders, would be precisely the sort of push needed to place flesh upon the now rather suspect concept of renewal as over against the polarization taking place in the churches.

It would be a gamble to believe a gracious act by church bureaucracy would trigger a new lay voluntarism, but it is a gamble worth taking. The resigned executives would certainly be capable of forming a new and progressive institution for the activist laity, should their departure have the negative effect of consolidating the denominations for the conservatives. The point is this. If denominational executives take the lead and are sincere in giving up their own power, they will be able to rally to their side forces silent since the civil rights movement died, to wrest by conflict, if necessary, the resources from denominations for purposes of reparation.

Amid the "new reformation" excursions of Forman and uptight white reaction to the rhetoric of the Black Manifesto, IFCO, the Interreligious Foundation for Community Organization, stands as the most important funnel through which ecclesiastical reparation funds might pass. And it may be helpful to outline something of IFCO, the Black Economic Development Conference, and the need for a clear understanding of what churches will face if there is no adequate response to the demand for black control of reparation funds.

Basically, IFCO is a channel for the funding of community

organization within the poor black-brown communities of the U.S. Founded in 1966 at the instigation of church executives, its membership now includes twenty-three organizations who have, through IFCO, funded some fifty community development projects with about $1.5 million. After approving a project, IFCO grants money in quarterly installments, each payment contingent on a financial and progress report from the project in question.

The IFCO Board includes major Protestant, Catholic and Jewish mission and social action agencies (or did before the American Jewish Committee pulled out); its directors number 20 blacks, 18 whites and one Mexican-American. According to Louis Gothard, IFCO's assistant director: "The Board's basic policy is that we do support mass-based community organizations. We've been able to . . . with the kinds of dollars that provide stuff for them to fight the battles they have in their own communities."

Lucius Walker, IFCO's director, conceived of the NBEDC (held in Detroit April 25–27) as an essential step in moving beyond a "parochial" notion of community organization to one including a broad strategy of economic development. There had, he maintained, been no wide consensus of black development strategy since the days of Booker T. Washington. So, as the Nixon Administration trimmed poverty programs and developed a rhetoric of black capitalism, IFCO funded the Detroit conference, in the words of Professor Robert Browne's keynote speech, with the hope of "developing a united position on at least some aspects of how we would like to see government and private money used in the black community."

Walker feels that the Detroit conference was held in order to be "taken over." That is, it had no prior agenda. The hope was that something like a strategy of action and consensus would emerge from the delegates themselves. James Forman had been invited as an official speaker, along with Julian Bond and other younger black activist leaders, and the Black Manifesto emerged with Forman. It was modified and changed to reflect emphases and ideas of other delegates at the conference. The notion of agricultural cooperatives in the South, reflected in the Manifesto's appeal for a southern land bank, was basically the proposal of Julian Bond.

Any assessment of the demands will reveal that they point to what is primarily a cultural program aimed at creating black unity and black power, and assuming that separatism is an essential ingredient in black development. Thus the 187–63 vote in favor of the Manifesto was not indicative of massive rejection either of its tone or spirit. There were, incidentally, an estimated one hundred abstentions.

Since the Detroit conference, black support of the Manifesto has increased, and the way has been opened for the development of white support as well. The occupation of Union Theological Seminary's administration buildings in May by white and black students was merely a prelude to expected support from white and black theological students.

After the Detroit conference, IFCO's board barred Lucius Walker and other staff members from participation in continuing organizations of the BEDC. This means that IFCO, while approving the Manifesto's demands in principle, can remain a broker between the white community and a broader spectrum of community action efforts than those proposed by the Manifesto. But now, because of reaction to James Forman's tactics, white churchmen seem desirous of stipulating that no money find its way to the BEDC, even though its programs will be guided by a steering committee containing men of the stature of Julian Bond and Vincent Harding. Indeed, there is even a question as to whether the churches will come up with the modest $270,000 that IFCO has pledged to raise to support the first phase of the BEDC's operations.

Lucius Walker is closer to the ghetto scene than the white executives who are being asked for the first time to sacrifice control over program moneys. IFCO neither funds nor supports the infinitesimally small number of militants who look toward exclusively violent strategies of change. In a recent response to false allegations of IFCO-militant ties by Los Angeles Police Sergeant Tobert Thoms, Walker noted: "Some of the groups we fund may well include black militants, but in our judgment this is where black militants should find the opportunity to participate with other citizens in redressing their grievances in society."

Churches that shy away from direct support of the BEDC and applaud the fact (as United Presbyterians did in their recent San Antonio General Assembly) that the white structure will retain full control of allocations to the black community are continuing a colonial mentality that can only stoke the fires of resentment and render the rhetoric of the Manifesto a reality.

At the moment IFCO is a plausible broker *between* the churches and black community. Failure to use IFCO, either by discrediting it or turning to white-controlled distribution programs, will be rightly seen as a manifestation of continuing white racism. Support of IFCO is a moderate step toward needed decolonization.

One of the most important developments is that Forman now has lines into churches through various black caucuses that have sprung up in white denominations and through the younger clergy of the black churches. But the fact remains that church campaigns for social action programs are not meeting quotas. To get $500 million there would have to be an actual transfer of existing assets, such as stock portfolios and real estate.

There is a good deal of desperation among younger churchmen of all colors. They find the church irrelevant but see few opportunities to effect social change through any other institutions. They may find the term "reparation" repugnant, but not self-determination for blacks. That just might give BEDC's crusade the momentum it needs.

DIVINE LIBEL

by DICK GREGORY

THE NATIONAL Black Economic Development Conference timed the attack upon the white churches and synagogues perfectly. The Black Manifesto was issued right after the Vatican pronouncement reevaluating the status of certain saints. Although immediate response to the $500 million reparation demand was not all that it could or should be, I understand a group of Roman Catholics decided to make modest reparation on their own and offered to send one million used St. Christopher medals to Harlem.

Basically, the Black Manifesto is an historical reminder to the white religious establishment. It points out the history of performance of white churches and synagogues and highlights the contradictions between words and deeds. Religious rhetoric has spoken of man's freedom and lifting the yoke of bondage, while the performance of the religious establishment has been to form an unholy alliance with a worldwide system of oppression.

The contradiction between words and deeds runs deep in the history of white Christianity. I got my first taste of that contradiction when I was very young. A white Christian minister came up to me one day and said, "Boy"—that's how I know he was a white Christian—"what do you want to do when you grow up?" I said, "Oh, Mr. White Christian, I wants to go to Africa and visit my ancestors!" With a look of pious horror, Mr. White Christian said, "Why would you want to have anything to do with those uncivilized people. Your ancestors are cannibals."

Reflecting my childhood innocence, I said, "Canni—who?"

"Cannibals, boy. Your ancestors eat folks."

"Ooooe! You mean they eat real live people?"

I was so shocked and ashamed that I followed Mr. White Christian into his church to pray. I fell on my knees and asked God to forgive my ancestors. "Please, God," I prayed, "forgive my ancestors for being so uncivilized that they eat people."

Mr. White Christian heard my prayer and came over to me. "We don't usually let colored boys in this church," he said. "But I like the way you pray. I want you to stay and have communion with us." Thank you, Mr. White Christian," I said, "But what's communion?" "Just get down on your knees and I'll show you," Mr. White Christian replied.

So I got down on my knees at the altar rail with the other folks, and Mr. White Christian handed me a piece of bread and a cup of grape juice and said, "This is his body and this is his blood." So I decided then and there I would have to amend my prayer to include many more people!

Observing the history of the performance of white Christian missionaries first aroused my curiosity about the strange power of the Bible. It seemed to me that the pattern was clear. When the white Christian missionaries went to Africa, the white folks had the bibles and the natives had the land. When the missionaries pulled out, they had the land and the natives had the bibles. Now that's a pretty good trick if you can pull it off. I've often wondered if I could try the same pattern with the Board of Directors of General Motors. I'd walk into the board meeting with my Bible under my arm. Naturally, the directors would own the corporation. If I could find the magic formula that worked so well for the missionaries, when I left the meeting, I'd own the corporation and each director would have a Bible.

The Black Manifesto seems to have no quarrel with the words of the Bible. It merely traces the history of colonization, oppression and economic exploitation which results wherever those words are read by the religious establishment.

Since the Bible has been used to exploit and the religious establishment has become wealthy, it is entirely just to demand that some of the wealth be divested back into the hands of the exploited. That's reparation in a nutshell.

Considering the history of economic exploitation and the vast stores of wealth held by the white churches and synagogues of this nation, the $500 million reparation demand of the National Black Economic Development Conference is a modest sum indeed. One cannot help wondering what God himself—the Boss of all Bosses—would demand if he ever took the religious establishment into court on charges of defamation of character. A divine libel action would surely demand a much larger sum from the churches for what they have been doing in God's name for the past twenty centuries.

Speaking through the prophet Amos, the Boss is on record concerning his feelings about religious folks who "trample upon the poor" and give certain sacred activities priority over the demands of justice. "I hate, I despise your feasts," said the prophet Amos, "and I take no delight in your solemn assemblies. . . . Take away from me the noise of your songs; to the melody of your harps I will not listen. But let justice roll down like waters, and righteousness like an overflowing stream."

Exhibit "A" in a divine libel action would no doubt be a selection of the most popular pictures of Jesus adorning the walls of church sanctuaries and Sunday School classrooms throughout the nation. What price would God demand from the churches for having the audacity to lighten the color of his son's skin, straighten out his nappy hair, and portray him as a clean white hippie in a suburban setting? Surely the Boss would "take no delight" in such adornments.

And surely the Boss would reject the songs and melodies of today's solemn assemblies. Church folks will gather in solemn assembly and sing the words, "Were you there when they crucified my Lord?" And when they sing those words, they have an expression on their faces that suggests that they *would* have been there—on the Hill of the Skull standing at the foot of the Cross—if they had the chance. But it is so cheap and easy to sing about what you *would* have done two thousand years too late. The question is what you *will* do and *are* doing right now.

When decent, thinking people lay their bodies on the line for their beliefs and truth and justice are crucified in the streets of this nation, are white church folks there in the same numbers as attend the solemn assemblies? If the Russians or Chinese took over this country tomorrow and rolled tanks into the streets and issued a decree that anyone caught going to church the following Sunday morning would be mowed down with machine guns, would most church folks attend? You know what would happen. Older church folk who never missed a day of church in their lives would wake up sick that Sunday morning. And, ironically, morally determined youth who never *attended* church in their lives would decide to worship that Sunday!

In their solemn assemblies, church folks will sing *The Battle Hymn of the Republic* and *Onward Christian Soldiers*. Remember the words? "As he *died* to make men holy, let us *die* to make men free." Church folks will sing those words and do just the reverse. They will *kill* and sanction killing to make men free. Church folks seem to believe that a "Christian soldier" is a Marine who prays! But that's a distortion for which the Boss would surely demand reparation. The words of both songs are really talking about a man who will follow the cause of right to his death.

But church folks will twist their religious language to justify almost anything. I came from a family where I was expected to go to church on Sunday. I used to sit next to so many people who *loved* God—until the chips were down. They were so busy *loving* God superficially that it never occurred to them to *respect* him and his word. My momma was like that. If she had respected God and the Bible, things would have been different at my house. The Ten Commandments clearly and unequivocally say, "Thou shalt not steal." Yet momma used to bring home food which she stole from the pantry of the white folks she was working for. She would cook it, serve it, and then *demand* that we kids pray over it. One day I took momma down into the basement where I hid the things I had stolen. I said, "Here, momma, You pray over what I have stolen and then I'll go back to the table and pray over what you have stolen." Momma didn't know that I was a better thief than she was. I just couldn't justify mine.

Then one day, when I was in my teens, I got caught snatching a pocketbook. I came back to my religious home and told momma what had happened. She went to the white folks and got a lawyer. The next day in court, my momma sat and watched me put my hand on that Bible which she said she loved. She heard me solemnly swear to tell "the truth, the whole truth, and nothing but the truth, so help me God." For the next two hours she listened to me lie to beat the case. And when that judge said, "Not guilty," my momma jumped up and shouted, "Thank God!" If that isn't using the Creator to justify stealing, I don't know what is. Testimony in a divine libel suit would no doubt be riddled with phrases like, "by their fruits you shall know them," highlighting the contradiction between word and deed in the religious establishment.

If the Boss took legal action against the religious establishment, he certainly would cite property holdings as a supreme example of "trampling upon the poor." The religious establishment is not only a wealthy property owner, but also enjoys a tax exempt status which places a larger tax burden upon the poor, those least able to afford any tax payment whatsoever. Nor has the religious community raised a united cry of moral indignation against the inequity of the tax structure in this country which allows the super-rich to escape tax payment through loopholes designed to protect wealth and power.

Many white church folks are morally indignant over the large numbers of black people, and other poor people, on relief. But they accept so easily the immorality of tax injustices in this country. I know about tax loopholes since I am in a high income bracket. It is possible for me to take an entire nightclub audience out for dinner, and it won't cost me a quarter because I can write off my income tax as publicity expense. Yet some poor white or black woman who needs to write off her baby's milk expense does not enjoy the same privilege.

The wealthiest families in this nation pay no income tax at

all. The hardest hit are middle-income taxpayers, those in the
$10,000-to-$20,000 bracket. The higher up the income bracket
a man climbs, the less tax he pays. Many millionaires in this
country pay absolutely no income tax. Oil depletion allowances
make it possible for big oil companies to earn a half-billion
dollars without paying a penny of taxes.

During his day in court, the Boss would surely read off a list
of church contributors (much like James Forman has done),
condemning the church's grateful acceptance of immoral
funds. The Mafia has always been known to pay its church
dues (although organized crime is as responsible as any other
single source for the continued misery of the poor).

New York State Senator John H. Hughes recently estimated
that $223 million is siphoned out of the New York City ghettos
of Central Harlem, the South Bronx and Bedford-Stuyvesant
annually by racketeers. He compared that statistic with an
estimated $272 million in welfare funds funneled into the
same areas by government agencies. Insisting that gambling
and narcotics peddling gives organized crime a stranglehold
on the ghettos, Senator Hughes said: "This hold is so tight that
until it is broken little by way of economic improvement can
be expected, no matter how much money and effort the state
devotes to the improvement of these areas."

A divine libel suit would surely "hate and despise" a religious establishment which can continue to build and decorate
buildings while human beings starve to death daily. Nor could
the Boss possibly approve of silence in the religious community while billions of dollars are sent to the moon and the
plates of America's hungry remain empty. It should be easier
to place food in a man's stomach than to place a man on the
moon. At least in the feeding process you have gravity working on your side.

Yet church folks rejoice in space exploration and enjoy
hearing the astronauts read the Bible to them from outer
space. The closest the religious establishment will get to really
being concerned about hunger is to advocate programs of
planned parenthood and, in protestantism at least, to push the
Pill in the world's ghettos.

But the Boss's Son said, "Feed my sheep." He didn't say

control the flock's reproduction. The Pill is merely an unnatural cop out to cover up the fact that about one-fourth of the world's land *could* be cultivated if money and training were made available by the haves to the have-nots. This land just simply is not used today. If it were, the world's food production would multiply four times. Even if the 10 percent of the world's land that *is* used for agriculture were *fully* utilized, ten times the present world population might be fed.

It is nature's law that man plants the seed to start the process of natural growth. It is true both of crop cultivation and human reproduction. With proper "seed" money, financial and technological commitment, the world could be fed and the Pill could be discarded as an unnatural resource.

Which leads to what would probably be the Boss's strongest indictment against the contemporary religious establishment. A divine libel suit would cite the religious community for failing to teach a proper respect for nature, which is the same, really, as teaching a respect for the divine. If man respected nature with a religious passion, he could not abuse her resources, pollute the natural environment and continue to undo creation through arrogant disrespect for human habitation.

If men were ever to become infused with a profound respect for nature, they would respect themselves and each other as nature's creatures. The Boss's Son hinted at that concept when he urged men to love their neighbors as *themselves*. That kind of self-love and self-respect would lead to an end of slaughter on the highways of America as well as on the battlefields of the world. And it would surely hasten the day when *all* forms of oppression and exploitation would be seen basically as expressions of self-denial opposed to the natural created order of life and leading ultimately only in the direction of self-destruction.

Yet the religious community consistently refused to embrace a concept of total respect for nature and nature's creatures. Some courageous members of the religious community will speak out against the war in Vietnam, or work to ban the bomb. But such actions are partial solutions when compared with the natural human problem. Church folks have the answer if they will only listen to it. "Thou shalt not kill." If church folks would believe that commandment, not only would they all become vegetarians, but they would see respect for nature in its proper perspective.

Personally, I am not opposed to war, nor am I opposed to the existence of national armies. But I believe the commandment. I am opposed to *killing*. Nations who feel that they must settle their differences through competitive combat may do so if that "war" does not involve killing. National leaders settling their differences at the chess or checkerboard would be a humane, even if risky, military strategy. Of course, competitive combat is never a lasting or even desirable solution. The power of right should stand on its own and should not need the representation of either military might or wit.

The presence of an army has value in a civilized nation, though a civilized military should not be involved in killing. An army is necessary, for example, to clean up after national disasters—hurricanes, tornadoes, floods, earthquakes, and the like. After every such natural disaster, the National Guard is called in to restore peace and order, to hold in check the looting and theft which always accompanies natural disorder. But that military function does not need to involve killing. The current irony in America is that the National Guard is called in after the "spontaneous combustion" of ghetto revolts but is ordered to kill rather than restore order, thus exacerbating a disaster rather than healing it.

The only road to world peace and to a climate of respect for nature is to render the concept of killing irrelevant. A peaceful world order cannot exist where any form of killing is allowed or justified. A world ban on capital punishment is more important than a ban on the bomb. Stop killing! That is the answer.

To talk of banning the bomb is pointless, because we already *have* the bomb. We might just as well urge men to "Forget the wheel." But if the idea of killing is eliminated from man's mind, the bomb will never be used. And if church folk were really concerned about escaping indictment in a divine libel action, they would be working to expand man's mind to envision a human order where killing has no place.

More important than petitions to ban the bomb are programs to feed a starving humanity, medical programs to heal a disease-ridden mankind, humanitarian approaches to world need which leave no time for military preoccupation.

Such a humanitarian world emphasis would lift the vision and enlist the energies of the new generation. The instinctive moral thirst of the youth of the world would be quenched. In years to come, youth would have been raised in an atmosphere enabling them to choose for themselves never again to drink of destruction, and the bomb will have been banned to its rightful status of irrelevance.

The Black Manifesto has caused the religious establishment in this country to feel the sting of indictment for past sins. But the white churches and synagogues should thank God that the indictment has been so restrained. If members of the religious community have any doubts about the justice of the reparation demand, they should try looking at themselves through the eyes of their Creator and doubt *would* fade into horror.

The Black Manifesto*

TO THE WHITE Christian Churches and the Synagogues in the United States of America and to All Other Racist Institutions:

Introduction: Total Control as the Only Solution to the Economic Problems of Black People

Brothers and Sisters:

We have come from all over the country burning with anger and despair not only with the miserable economic plight of our people but fully aware that the racism on which the Western World was built dominates our lives. There can be no separation of the problems of racism from the problems of our economic, political, and cultural degradation. To any black man, this is clear.

But there are still some of our people who are clinging to the rhetoric of the Negro, and we must separate ourselves from these Negroes who go around the country promoting all types of schemes for black capitalism.

Ironically, some of the most militant Black Nationalists, as they call themselves, have been the first to jump on the bandwagon of black capitalism. They are pimps; black power pimps and fraudulent leaders, and the people must be educated to

---

* This document was presented by James Forman to the National Black Economic Development Conference in Detroit, Michigan, and adopted on April 26, 1969.

understand that any black man or Negro who is advocating a perpetuation of capitalism inside the United States is in fact seeking not only his ultimate destruction and death but is contributing to the continuous exploitation of black people all around the world. For it is the power of the United States Government, this racist, imperialist government, that is choking the life of all people around the world.

We are an African people. We sit back and watch the Jews in this country make Israel a powerful conservative state in the Middle East, but we are not concerned actively about the plight of our brothers in Africa. We are the most advanced technological group of black people in the world, and there are many skills that could be offered to Africa. At the same time, it must be publicly stated that many African leaders are in disarray themselves, having been duped into following the lines as laid out by the western imperialist governments. Africans themselves succumbed to and are victims of the power of the United States. For instance, during the summer of 1967, as the representatives of SNCC, Howard Moore and I traveled extensively in Tanzania and Zambia. We talked to high, very high, government officials. We told them there were many black people in the United States who were willing to come and work in Africa. All these government officials, who were part of the leadership in their respective governments, said they wanted us to send as many skilled people as we could contact. But this program never came into fruition, and we do not know the exact reasons, for I assure you that we talked and were committed to making this a successful program. It is our guess that the United States put the squeeze on these countries, for such a program directed by SNCC would have been too dangerous to the international prestige of the United States. It is also possible that some of the wild statements by some black leader frightened the Africans.

In Africa today there is a great suspicion of black people in this country. This is a correct suspicion since most of the Negroes who have left the States for work in Africa usually work for the Central Intelligence Agency (CIA) or the State Department. But the respect for us as a people continues to mount, and the day will come when we can return to our homeland as brothers and sisters. But we should not think of going back to Africa today, for we are located in a strategic position. We live inside the United States, which is the most barbaric country in the world, and we have a chance to help bring this government down.

Time is short, and we do not have much time and it is time we stop mincing words. Caution is fine, but no oppressed people ever gained their liberation until they were ready to fight, to use whatever means necessary, including the use of force and power of the gun to bring down the colonizer.

We have heard the rhetoric, but we have not heard the rhetoric which says that black people in this country must understand that we are the vanguard force. We shall liberate all the people in the United States, and we will be instrumental in the liberation of colored people the world around. We must understand this point very clearly so that we are not trapped into diversionary and reactionary movements. Any class analysis of the United States shows very clearly that black people are the most oppressed group of people inside the United States. We have suffered the most from racism and exploitation, cultural degradation and lack of political power. It follows from the laws of revolution that the most oppressed will make the revolution, but we are not talking about just making the revolution. All the parties on the left who consider themselves revolutionary will say that blacks are the vanguard, but we are saying that not only are we the vanguard, but we must assume leadership, total control, and we must exercise the humanity which is inherent in us. We are the most humane people within the United States. We have suffered and we understand suffering. Our hearts go out to the Vietnamese, for we know what it is to suffer under the domination of racist America. Our hearts, our soul and all the compassion we can mount go out to our brothers in Africa, Santa Domingo, Latin America and Asia who are being tricked by the power structure of the United States which is dominating the world today. These ruthless, barbaric men have systematically tried to kill all people and organizations opposed to its imperialism. We no longer can just get by with the use of the word capitalism to describe the United States, for it is an imperial power sending money, missionaries and the army throughout the world to protect this government and the few rich whites who control it. General Motors and all the major auto industries are operating in South Africa, yet the white dominated leadership of the United Auto Workers sees no relationship to the exploitation of the black people in South Africa and the exploitation of black people in the United States. If they understand it, they certainly do not put it into practice, which is the actual test. We as black people must be concerned with the total conditions of all black people in the world.

But while we talk of revolution, which will be an armed confrontation and long years of sustained guerilla warfare inside this country, we must also talk of the type of world we want to live in. We must commit ourselves to a society where the total means of production are taken from the rich and placed into the hands of the state for the welfare of all the people. This is what we mean when we say total control. And we mean that black people who have suffered the most from exploitation and racism must move to protect their black interest by assuming leadership inside of the United States of everything that exists. The time has ceased when we are second in command and the white boy stands on top. This is especially true of the welfare agencies in this country, but it is not enough to say that a black man is on top. He must be committed to building the new society, to taking the wealth away from the rich people, such as General Motors, Ford, Chrysler, the DuPonts, the Rockefellers, the Mellons, and all the other rich white exploiters and racists who run this world.

Where do we begin? We have already started. We started the moment we were brought to this country. In fact, we started on the shores of Africa, for we have always resisted attempts to make us slaves, and now we must resist the attempts to make us capitalists. It is in the financial interest of the United States to make us capitalist, for this will be the same line as that of integration into the mainstream of American life. Therefore, brothers and sisters, there is no need to fall into the trap that we have to get an ideology. We HAVE an ideology. Our fight is against racism, capitalism and imperialism, and we are dedicated to building a socialist society inside the United States where the total means of production and distribution are in the hands of the State, and that must be led by black people, by revolutionary blacks who are concerned about the total humanity of this world. And, therefore, we obviously are different from some of those who seek a black nation in the United States, for there is no way for that nation to be viable if in fact the United States remains in the hands of white racists. Then too, let us deal with some arguments that we should share power with whites. We say that there must be a revolutionary black vanguard, and that white people in this country must be willing to accept black leadership, for that is the only protection that black people have to protect ourselves from racism rising again in this country.

Racism in the United States is so pervasive in the mentality of whites that only an armed, well-disciplined, black-controlled government can insure the stamping out of racism in this country. And that is why we plead with black people not to be talking about a few crumbs, a few thousand dollars for this cooperative, or a thousand dollars which splits black people into fighting over the dollar. That is the intention of the government. We say . . . think in terms of total control of the United States. Prepare ourselves to seize state power. Do not hedge, for time is short, and all around the world the forces of liberation are directing their attacks against the United States. It is a powerful country, but that power is not greater than that of black people. We work the chief industries in this country, and we could cripple the economy while the brothers fought guerilla warfare in the streets. This will take some long range planning, but whether it happens in a thousand years is of no consequence. It cannot happen unless we start. How then is all of this related to this conference?

First of all, this conference is called by a set of religious people, Christians, who have been involved in the exploitation and rape of black people since the country was founded. The missionary goes hand in hand with the power of the states. We must begin seizing power wherever we are, and we must say to the planners of this conference that you are no longer in charge. We the people who have assembled here thank you for getting us here, but we are going to assume power over the conference and determine from this moment on the direction which we want it to go. We are not saying that the conference was planned badly. The staff of the conference has worked hard and has done a magnificent job in bringing all of us together, and we must include them in the new membership which must surface from this point on. The conference is now the property of the people who are assembled here. This we proclaim as fact and not rhetoric, and there are demands that we are going to make and we insist that the planners of this conference help us implement them.

We maintain we have the revolutionary right to do this. We have the same rights, if you will, as the Christians had in going into Africa and raping our Motherland and bringing us away from our continent of peace and into this hostile and alien environment where we have been living in perpetual warfare since 1619.

Our seizure of power at this conference is based on a program, and our program is contained in the following Manifesto:

Black Manifesto

We the black people assembled in Detroit, Michigan, for the National Black Economic Development Conference are fully aware that we have been forced to come together because racist white America has exploited our resources, our minds, our bodies, our labor. For centuries we have been forced to live as colonized people inside the United States, victimized by the most vicious, racist system in the world. We have helped to build the most industrialized country in the world.

We are therefore demanding of the white Christian churches and Jewish synagogues, which are part and parcel of the system of capitalism, that they begin to pay reparations to black people in this country. We are demanding $500,000,000 from the Christian white churches and the Jewish synagogues. This total comes to fifteen dollars per nigger. This is a low estimate, for we maintain there are probably more than 30,000,000 black people in this country. Fifteen dollars a nigger is not a large sum of money, and we know that the churches and synagogues have a tremendous wealth and its membership, white America, has profited and still exploits black people. We are also not unaware that the exploitation of colored peoples around the world is aided and abetted by the white Christian churches and synagogues. This demand for $500,000,000 is not an idle resolution or empty words. Fifteen dollars for every black brother and sister in the United States is only a beginning of the reparations due us as people who have been exploited and degraded, brutalized, killed and persecuted. Underneath all of this exploitation, the racism of this country has produced a psychological effect upon us that we are beginning to shake off. We are no longer afraid to demand our full rights as a people in this decadent society.

We are demanding $500,000,000 to be spent in the following way:

(1) We call for the establishment of a southern land bank to help our brothers and sisters who have to leave their land because of racist pressure, and for people who want to establish cooperative farms but who have no funds. We have seen too many farmers evicted from their homes because they have dared to defy the white racism of this country. We need money for land. We must fight for massive sums of money for this southern land bank. We call for $200,000,000 to implement this program.

(2) We call for the establishment of four major publishing and printing industries in the United States to be funded with ten million dollars each. These publishing houses are to be located in Detroit, Atlanta, Los Angeles, and New York. They will help to generate capital for further cooperative investments in the black community, provide jobs and an alternative to the white-dominated and controlled printing field.

(3) We call for the establishment of four of the most advanced scientific and futuristic audio-visual networks to be located in Detroit, Chicago, Cleveland and Washington, D.C. These TV networks will provide an alternative to the racist propaganda that fills the current television networks. Each

of these TV networks will be funded by ten million dollars each.

(4) We call for a research skills center which will provide research on the problems of black people. This center must be funded with no less than thirty million dollars.

(5) We call for the establishment of a training center for the teaching of skills in community organization, photography, movie making, television making and repair, radio building and repair and all other skills needed in communication. This training center shall be funded with no less than ten million dollars.

(6) We recognize the role of the National Welfare Rights Organization, and we intend to work with them. We call for ten million dollars to assist in the organization of welfare recipients. We want to organize welfare workers in this country so that they may demand more money from the government and better administration of the welfare system of this country.

(7) We call for $20,000,000 to establish a National Black Labor Strike and Defense Fund. This is necessary for the protection of black workers and their families who are fighting racist working conditions in this country.

(8) We call for the establishment of the International Black Appeal (IBA). This International Black Appeal will be funded with no less than $20,000,000. The IBA is charged with producing more capital for the establishment of cooperative businesses in the United States and in Africa, our Motherland. The International Black Appeal is one of the most important demands that we are making, for we know that it can generate and raise funds throughout the United States and help our African brothers. The IBA is charged with three functions and shall be headed by James Forman:

(a) Raising money for the program of the National Black Economic Development Conference.
(b) The development of cooperatives in African countries and support of African liberation movements.
(c) Establishment of a Black Anti-Defamation League which will protect our African image.

(9) We call for the establishment of a black university to be founded with $130,000,000, to be located in the South. Negotiations are presently under way with a southern university.

(10) We demand that IFCO allocate all unused funds in the planning budget to implement the demands of this conference.

In order to win our demands, we are aware that we will have to have massive support, therefore:

(1) We call upon all black people throughout the United States to consider themselves as members of the National Black Economic Development Conference and to act in unity to help force the racist white Christian churches and Jewish synagogues to implement these demands.

(2) We call upon all the concerned black people across the country to contact black workers, black women, black students and the black unemployed, community groups, welfare organizations, teachers' organizations, church leaders and organizations, explaining how these demands are vital to the black community of the United States. Pressure by whatever means necessary should be applied to the white power structure. All black people should act boldly in confronting our white oppressors and demanding this modest reparation of fifteen dollars per black man.

(3) Delegates and members of the National Black Economic Development Conference are urged to call press conferences in the cities and to attempt to get as many black organizations as possible to support the demands of the conference. The quick use of the press in the local areas will heighten the tension, and these demands must be attempted to be won in a short period of time, although we are prepared for protracted and long-range struggle.

(4) We call for the total disruption of selected church-sponsored agencies operating anywhere in the United States and the world. Black workers, black women, black students and the black unemployed are encouraged to seize the offices, telephones, and printing apparatus of all church-sponsored agencies and to hold these in trusteeship until our demands are met.

(5) We call upon all delegates and members of the National Black Economic Development Conference to stage sit-in demonstrations at selected black and white churches. This is not to be interpreted as a continuation of the sit-in movement of the early sixties, but we know that active confrontation inside white churches is possible and will strengthen the possibility of meeting our demands. Such confrontation can take the form of reading the Black Manifesto instead of a sermon, or passing it out to church members. The principle of self-defense should be applied if attacked.

(6) On May 4, 1969, or a date thereafter, depending upon local conditions, we call upon black people to commence the disruption of the racist churches and synagogues throughout the United States.

(7) We call upon IFCO to serve as a central staff to coordinate the mandate of the conference and to reproduce and distribute en masse literature, leaflets, news items, press releases and other material.

(8) We call upon all delegates to find within the white community those forces which will work under the leadership of blacks to implement these demands by whatever means necessary. By taking such actions, white Americans will demonstrate concretely that they are willing to fight the white skin privilege and the white supremacy and racism which has forced us as black people to make these demands.

(9) We call upon all white Christians and Jews to practice patience, tolerance, understanding and nonviolence as they have been encouraged, advised and demanded that we as black people should do throughout our entire enforced slavery in the United States. The true test of their faith and belief in the Cross and the words of the prophets will certainly be put to a test as we seek legitimate and extremely modest reparations for our role in developing the industrial base of the western world through our slave labor. But we are no longer slaves, we are men and women, proud of our African heritage, determined to have our dignity.

(10) We are so proud of our African heritage and realize concretely that our struggle is not only to make revolution in the United States but to protect our brothers and sisters in

Africa and to help them rid themselves of racism, capitalism and imperialism by whatever means necessary, including armed struggle. We are and must be willing to fight the defamation of our African image wherever it rears its ugly head. We are therefore charging the steering committee to create a black Anti-Defamation League to be founded by money raised from the International Black Appeal.

(11) We fully recognize that revolution in the United States and Africa, our Motherland, is more than a one dimensional operation. It will require the total integration of the political, economic and military components, and therefore we call upon all our brothers and sisters who have acquired training and expertise in the fields of engineering, electronics, research, community organization, physics, biology, chemistry, mathematics, medicine, military science and warfare to assist the National Black Economic Development Conference in the implementation of its program.

(12) To implement these demands we must have a fearless leadership. We must have a leadership which is willing to battle the church establishment to implement these demands. To win our demands we will have to declare war on the white Christian churches and synagogues, and this means we may have to fight the total government structure of this country. Let no one here think that these demands will be met by our mere stating them. For the sake of the churches and synagogues, we hope that they have the wisdom to understand that these demands are modest and reasonable. But if the white Christians and Jews are not willing to meet our demands through peace and goodwill, then we declare war, and we are prepared to fight by whatever means necessary. We are, therefore, proposing the election of the following steering committee: *

Lucius Walker	*Mark Comfort*
Renny Freeman	*Earl Allen*
Luke Tripp	*Robert Browne*
Howard Fuller	*Vincent Harding*

* (This list was later revised, more Church representatives were added— eds.)

James Forman	Mike Hamlin
John Watson	Len Holt
Dan Aldridge	Peter Bernard
John Williams	Michael Wright
Ken Cockrel	Muhammed Kenyatta
Chuck Wooten	Mel Jackson
Fannie Lou Hamer	Howard Moore
Julian Bond	Harold Homes

Brothers and sisters, we are no longer shuffling our feet and scratching our heads. We are tall, black and proud.

And we say to the white Christian churches and Jewish synagogues, to the government of this country and to all the white racist imperialists who compose it, there is only one thing left that you can do to further degrade black people and that is to kill us. But we have been dying too long for this country. We have died in every war. We are dying in Vietnam today fighting the wrong enemy.

The new black man wants to live, and to live means that we must not become static or merely believe in self-defense. We must boldly go out and attack the white Western world at its power centers. The white Christian churches are another form of government in this country, and they are used by the government of this country to exploit the people of Latin America, Asia and Africa, but the day is soon coming to an end. Therefore, brothers and sisters, the demands we make upon the white Christian churches and the Jewish synagogues are small demands. They represent fifteen dollars per black person in these United States. We can legitimately demand this from the church power structure. We must demand more from the United States Government.

But to win our demands from the church, which is linked up with the United States Government, we must not forget that it will ultimately be by force and power that we will win.

We are not threatening the churches. We are saying that we know the churches came with the military might of the colonizers and have been sustained by the military might of the colonizers. Hence, if the churches in colonial territories were established by military might, we know deep within our hearts that we must be prepared to use force to get our demands. We are not saying that this is the road we want to take. It is not, but let us be very clear that we are not opposed to force and we are not opposed to violence. We were captured in Africa by violence. We were kept in bondage and political servitude and forced to work as slaves by the military machinery and the Christian Church working hand in hand.

We recognize that in issuing this Manifesto we must prepare for a long-range educational campaign in all communities of this country, but we know that the Christian churches have contributed to our oppression in white America. We do not intend to abuse our black brothers and sisters in black churches who have uncritically accepted Christianity. We want them to understand how the racist white Christian church with its hypocritical declarations and doctrines of brotherhood has abused our trust and faith. An attack on the religious beliefs of black people is not our major objective, even though we know that we were not Christians when we were brought to this country, but that Christianity was used to help enslave us. Our objective in issuing this Manifesto is to force the racist white Christian church to begin the payment of reparations which are due to all black people, not only by the church but also by private business and the United States government. We see this focus on the Christian church as an effort around which all black people can unite.

Our demands are negotiable, but they cannot be minimized, they can only be increased, and the church is asked to come up with larger sums of money than we are asking. Our slogans are:

> *All Roads Must Lead to Revolution*
> *Unite with Whomever You Can Unite*
> *Neutralize Wherever Possible*
> *Fight Our Enemies Relentlessly*
> *Victory to the People*
> *Life and Good Health to Mankind*
> *Resistance to Domination by the White Christian Churches*
> *and the Jewish Synagogues*
> *Revolutionary Black Power*
> *We Shall Win Without a Doubt*

What Shall Our Response Be?
Riverside Speaks First

by Dr. Ernest Campbell*

LAST SUNDAY MORNING, May 4, our church was given a rude and jarring insight into the reality of life outside its walls. It isn't that we hadn't known and ministered to that world before. Riverside's record as a church that cares and dares is beyond dispute by any objective standard. It was simply that on Sunday last we became aware of the intensity of the bitterness that some members of the black community feel toward institutions that belong to the establishment, particularly the church.

The interruption of our service of Holy Communion that Sunday was first page news across the country. Whether the incident should have received such play from the press is a moot question. At any rate, it happened—Riverside Church was confronted with a Manifesto and a series of demands by the National Black Economic Development Conference. We didn't want it. We didn't welcome it. But we got it.

* The Riverside Church, a noted interdenominational, interracial congregation in New York's Morningside Heights, was the first religious institution in the nation to receive specific demands from the NBEDC. And it was the first to respond. Mr. Forman asked, during a worship interruption, for 60 percent of the church's annual income, a list of assets, free office space, classrooms for use of Harlem residents and unrestricted black use of the church's WRVR-FM radio station twelve hours a day and weekends. Doctor Campbell, preaching minister of Riverside, responded on the evening of May 10 in a WRVR broadcast. His remarks are reprinted with permission.

You can well imagine that our mail was heavy this week and our telephone lines warm. I appreciate very much the notes and letters of encouragement that members and friends of Riverside were kind enough to write. But the mail was not all local. From every section in these States people wrote, phoned or wired to make their feelings known. When anybody tampers with the church the country twitches and the hearts of many are revealed.

The tone of the overwhelming majority of those calls and letters? "We're sorry it happened. Sock it to 'em." Some of the letters were so hot they should have been sealed in asbestos. The predominant reaction to what happened at Riverside on the 4th of May can be summed up in five words: "The Shame Of It All." "The Shame Of It All."

I agreed. But wherein lay the shame? Was it that corporate worship, a "top sacred" part of man's life, had been desecrated by an illegal and hostile interruption? Let's be careful here— our hypocrisy may be showing. If worship means all that much to us, how come the majority of Christians in this country attend only when it suits them? Most church sanctuaries in this country could not seat their membership. Worship doesn't mean all that much to the average member. We sense that it *should*, but we know that it *doesn't*.

No, the shame of it all was not that a service of worship was interrupted, indefensible as that action was. The shame centers in the fact that within the population of this most prosperous nation there are people who feel, rightly or wrongly, that they have to use such tactics to draw attention to their grievances.

The Church's Response

Riverside Church has been busy working out a response to the needs behind the demands of the National Black Economic Development Conference. The ministers gathered daily. Council VII, responsible for the church's social relations, has met on the subject. Trustees and Deacons have been busy with it. Some of Riverside's black members have sat down with it as a group. We have been in touch with many ministers who serve the urban community. It would be hard to imagine a member of Riverside who hasn't thought about his church this week. I hope all of you have prayed.

What then is our response? First, we want to develop to an even greater degree than we have in the past an adequate forum where yeasty ideas can be expounded and debated, including the ideas contained in the Manifesto delivered to us last week. We do not believe, however, that a service of divine worship is the context best suited to this purpose. We affirm our belief in the integrity of worship and will not suffer our services to be wantonly interrupted by every individual who sees himself a champion of some worthy cause.

To this end we have received from the courts a Civil Restraining Order that could place any individual in contempt of court who interfered with our worship of Almighty God or otherwise sought to render the Riverside Church inoperative. This includes anyone who would rise to speak without prior arrangement, any who attempt to bring television cameras or flash cameras into the Nave or Chancel, any in the congregation, members and non-members alike, whose conduct in the pews threatened the service. It goes without saying that this order does not bar anyone from entering the church or worshipping. It protects against disruption.

We strongly believe that the help of the Police Department should be invoked only as a last resort. But such help will be sought if needed. The church when it is gathered for worship is particularly vulnerable to assault. Unlike university campuses where the dominant age range is 18 to 28, the average congregation reaches from young children to elderly men and women. Many are not strong of hand or nimble of foot. All must be protected. We ask those who come to worship with us tomorrow to come as to the Lord's house with calm minds and hearts composed in love.

Many of those who volunteered their counsel to Riverside this week exhorted us to deal harshly with the man who intruded himself upon us Sunday, May 4, in the name of the National Black Economic Development Conference. While we have no intention of allowing him to exact extortion from the church and find his demands upon Riverside Church absurd and fanciful, we will not make of him a villain and thus artfully dodge the truth that underlies his cause. And that truth as our consciences should have told us for years, and the Kerner Report told us fourteen months ago, is that our society is suffering from the blight of racism. The churches of the land, far from being a vigorous part of the solution of this problem, have been apathetic beneficiaries of it.

Let's be done with rationalizing. Wherever you go in this country the white man rides higher than the black. He lives in the better parts of town, sends his children to more desirable schools, borrows books from finer libraries, holds down higher paying jobs. In the rice paddies of Vietnam more blacks are dying proportionately than whites, because the draft laws that prevail favor the white youth who can make it to college over the disadvantaged black youth who cannot.

And where has the church been in all of this? By its silence it has blessed these arrangements and given them an aura of divine approval. It has conveniently exalted the virtues of obedience and order—getting fat in the process. It has forgotten the poor and the dispirited.

When the church refuses to follow her Lord into the busy thoroughfares of history, when it talks of love but fails to press for basic justice, when its message has no other focus than the well-being of individual souls and lacks all public reference, when it refuses to put its own power on the line on behalf of the disadvantaged, when it lowers its voice in order to raise its budget, when it becomes more concerned to perpetuate and adorn its life than to lose its life for the sake of Christ and the gospel—when all of this happens, as it has, the church can be rightly changed with contributing to the social and economic inequities that provoke minorities to violence.

What of Reparations?

The word "reparations" has come up frequently of late. The latest edition of the Random House Dictionary gives as the first meaning of the term, "The making of amends for wrong or injury done." From the beginning the Christian church has taught that restitution is an essential part of penitence. You don't simply say "I'm sorry" to a man you've robbed. You return what you stole or your apology takes on a hollow ring.

Reparations, restitution, redress, call it what you will. We subscribe to the conviction that given the demeaning and heinous mistreatment that black people suffered in this country at the hands of white people in the slave economy, and given the lingering handicaps of that system that still work to keep the black man at a disadvantage in our society, it is just and reasonable that amends be made by many institutions in society—including, and perhaps especially, the church.

The Riverside Church, long committed to the struggle for civil rights, has determined through its Board of Deacons to make a fixed percentage of its annual budget available to a fund to be set apart for the rapid improvement of all disadvantaged people in this country. It is our hope that this fund will become national in scope and we respectfully invite churches and synagogues across the country to join us in the planning and funding of this venture. Care must be taken to see that the funds contributed are spent and administered at the discretion of responsible and representative leaders of the people the fund would help.

We call upon other institutions to come forward in a similar way—foundations, denominations, business corporations and government. Good and exciting things can happen. There is no plausible reason why a nation of this magnitude could not get at poverty once and for all had it the will to do so.

The radio station of The Riverside Church, WRVR, has from the beginning been sensitive to the issues that tear at the fabric of society. Several weeks ago the committee responsible for this station began considering the possibility of making a substantial body of time available to responsible and representative groups in the black and Spanish communities for the kind of programming they want to produce and hear. This possibility will become a reality at the earliest possible date.

The Riverside Church has always been open to responsible suggestions as to how its program could be improved and its outreach more helpfully extended. We are as open now as ever.

What of Revolution?

The Manifesto currently being presented to the churches and synagogues of the United States asserts that revolution is the only remedy for our social ills. Obviously, we reject this point of view. It may well be that the insurrectionist tone of the Manifesto is meant as an attention-getting ploy and not to be taken at literal face value. It would be helpful if the Interfaith Foundation For Community Organization, a principal sponsor of the National Black Economic Development Conference, would clarify this point for us and other churches and synagogues across the country. At the same time we believe that when desperate people talk this way, intransigence and rigidity on the part of the establishment only tend to prove the revolutionary's point—that the situation is hopeless. By pursuing justice for others as heartily as we prize it for ourselves, we weaken the revolutionary's case, improve the lot of our brother and glorify God.

The days through which we pass are heavy and hard for all of us. It is imperative that we rise in the strength of the living God to the highest that we know and not succumb to a mean and divisive spirit. Many in our society have stood in line for years, hat in hand, waiting for justice and a fair chance at a full and happy life. Their mood has understandably shifted from passive forebearance to angry and militant insistence. The new tactics are shocking and abrasive. They are designed to get our attention and rouse us from our lethargy. Let us react to the need and not confuse the issue by over-reacting to the tactics.

The gospel of Jesus Christ is still the power of God unto salvation. When love combines with justice what can stand before it? Let us as a people set a good example for other churches in the land by committing ourselves afresh to what we hold to be the aim of all our striving—"to do justly, to love mercy, and to walk humbly with our God."

APPENDIX 3

IFCO and the Crisis of American Society

by Lucius Walker*

THE INTERRELIGIOUS FOUNDATION for Community Organization
—IFCO as we are known—has become almost a household
word. There are two reasons for this.

One is the negative attack made on Christian and Jewish
agencies which created IFCO to coordinate their community
organization efforts. I shall deal with this situation first.

I am referring in this first instance to the charges made
(this week) by Los Angeles Police Sergeant Robert Thoms
(before a meeting of private police agencies funded by a
publishing house known for its ultra-conservative publications) in a speech before the international security conference
in Chicago. Sergeant Thoms made these "disclosures":

(1) "that hundreds of thousands of dollars" of church
money has gone to black militants in Chicago and
throughout the nation.

(2) that IFCO is under federal investigation because of
contributions to militants.

(3) that his investigation has turned up names of several
organizations funded by IFCO for $885,831 and dis-
persed by IFCO since its formation, with about 83

* The Reverend Lucius Walker is director of the Interreligious Foundation for Community Organization. The contents of this document were
presented in an informal session during the American Baptist Convention, his denomination, on May 17, 1969, in Seattle, Washington. It is
reprinted with permission.

percent of that "granted to community groups involved in militant or disruptive activities."

Thoms said all this is "an example of tax exempt money being utilized for noncharitable organizations spent on destroying what America believes in." He also said his attack was not on the churches, "but I would like to draw attention to the fact that church people may unwittingly be falling into sentimental traps and are not careful enough about where they're putting their money." He named ten organizations as members of IFCO and "disclosed" that six of the member groups of IFCO are prime members of the National Council of Churches.

(First, I want to answer the charges made by Sergeant Thoms, then I will go on to tell you about the dangers to our freedom posed by such blatant misuse of police powers as those demonstrated by Sergeant Thoms within the last week.) In spite of his claims that he has conducted an intensive investigation, the information which Sergeant Thoms called "disclosures" is information which was obtainable from public records distributed by IFCO announcing its income and its grant expenditures. That information is itself outdated and therefore misrepresents the facts. IFCO has long since exceeded $885,831 in disbursements. A more accurate figure is 1.5 million dollars. The last time IFCO had only ten member agencies was in October of 1967. Since that time, our membership list has steadily increased until now IFCO comprises twenty-three different agencies. It is no secret that more than six of those member agencies are members of the National Council of Churches. It is also no secret that the National Council of Churches is itself not a member agency of IFCO and, while IFCO has been endorsed and its program supported by the National Council of Churches, there is no official relationship between the National Council of Churches and the Interreligious Foundation for Community Organization.

It is highly improper for a police official to traffic in such vicious half-truths and innuendo. If the Los Angeles police intelligence division had or has any substantial evidence of illegal activity by IFCO, it then has an obligation to make this known to the public. Instead Mr. Thoms has chosen to use slander rather than fact. If any police official has substantial evidence of the use of IFCO grants by grantees for illegal activity, he might perform a useful public service by making such information known to us and to the public. Mr. Thoms, however, has never talked to our office. In spite of his claim that he has conducted an intensive investigation, he has neither sought information from nor given any information to this office. The only information he "discovered" was a public report issued by our office of public information.

Mr. Thoms has intimated that, but for his so-called "disclosure" of funds allocated by IFCO to community groups, that information would not have been forthcoming. That is simply not true. I would like to make it very clear that IFCO's policy since September 1967, when the foundation began its work, has been to make available to the public-at-large information about our finances. We have periodically distributed public reports, news releases to religious and secular press and magazine articles on amounts and sources of income, administrative expenses and grants made. No secret has ever been made of the groups IFCO has funded, how much they were granted, or for what purposes. Moreover, we have cancelled grants whenever we learned that agreements stipulated in our contracts with a grantee were not being fulfilled. So you see Mr. Thoms has not only misled the public. I believe he has insulted the public's intelligence by pretending to have information no one else had.

(As long as Mr. Thoms feels motivated to distribute information about IFCO, we wish he would use up-to-date information which shows that IFCO has allocated grants totaling 1.5 million to about fifty groups around the country, and that we have twenty-three member groups, not ten. The irony of Thoms' so-called "disclosures" are that he uses one and a half-year-old information taken from IFCO's own public statements.) I would also like to make it very clear that IFCO funds have not gone exclusively to militant groups. Our funds go to projects that are inclusive in their membership and promote people power so that poor minority persons can redress their grievances in society. The groups we fund represent diverse segments of community population ranging from conservative to militant. The types of projects we fund are also diverse, including such activities as tutorial projects, job training, voter education, housing and recreation. Some of the groups we fund may well include black militants, but in our judgment this is where black militants should find the opportunity to participate with other citizens in redressing their grievances in society.

Certainly all efforts undertaken by groups we have funded have not been totally successful, either by their standards or ours. On balance, however, we have made fewer mistakes than the average police department in this country and fewer mistakes than many space and medical research efforts which have wasted millions of dollars in following pipe dreams that never paid off. Not until this country realizes that it must do more in the high risk area of human development than in moon, space, ocean and esoteric projects will we solve the difficult human problem that confronts us.

Mr. Thoms' statements obviously were intended as a political attack, and he distorts the record. But let me set it straight: the claim that we are connected with the Black Panther Party is utterly ridiculous. The charges made in the Thoms' statement demonstrate a threat to this society's commitment to voluntarism, pluralism and participatory democracy.

To my knowledge all people involved in IFCO do indeed believe in the police. We support our local police in their proper place and in the assumption of their proper responsibility to society. In my judgment, however, Mr. Thoms' statements point up the dangerous tendency ·in our society of police officers to exercise power far in excess of their traditional role. On the face of it, it would appear that when a police sergeant is in a position to make wild and unfounded, irresponsible charges and proceed to announce a federal investigation almost as a matter of personal promise, every American citizen should be alarmed. Certainly his announcements and promise of a federal investigation implies a dubious collusion between government and law enforcement officials, and that is a serious business which threatens the very foundation stone of American society—the doctrine of separation of governmental powers.

The second development which has resulted in IFCO's becoming very much of a household word (within the last few weeks) has been the creative leadership exercised by IFCO in the convening of a three-day session called a National Black Economic Development Conference. In September 1968, the IFCO Board of Directors, determining that it could make a significant contribution to the developments of black communities by convening a forum within which there could be full, free discussion of the concerns of a wide range of black citizens on matters affecting economic development of black communities, authorized the funding of such a conference.

More than 500 persons registered for that conference, exceeding the expected three to four hundred registrants. Attendance throughout the week totaled an estimated seven to eight hundred. In our judgment, this represents a degree of interest in the black community in its economic development which fully justified the earlier IFCO position that such a conference was timely.

Throughout the conference, speakers and participants concurred in total consensus on such points as the irrelevance of black capitalism as a political slogan, which is intended to further coopt and compromise the black community, the dysfunction of capitalist interest in contributing to the genuine liberation of the black community, and thirdly, an impatience with piecemeal programmatic projects for the economic development of the black community. There were repeated calls for comprehensive programs that would have addressed themselves to total control of black communities by black people. These points were contained in many conference workshop and caucus resolutions and were reiterated in a document that was presented on Saturday evening, titled: "Total Control of Black Communities—The Only Solution to the Black Economic Development," by Mr. James Forman. At the close of this speech, Mr. Forman presented a document that has since become known as the "Black Manifesto" in which reparations in the total of 500 million dollars from white Christian churches and synagogues was demanded for nine specific programmatic purposes. (Mr. Walker here listed the program plans as contained in the Manifesto—eds.)

After full and lively discussion, the vote on the adoption of that Manifesto as an official document of the conference was passed by a vote of 3 to 1. The Manifesto called for the establishment of a steering committee and a follow-up organization that would continue beyond the three-day meeting to be known by the same name, i.e., The National Black Economic Development Conference.

IFCO applauds itself and feels that its responsibility as a community organization foundation has been justly exercised in convening the forum where such a new thrust could emanate. In board action taken in a special called meeting following the National Black Economic Development Conference, the Board of Directors of IFCO adopted the following statement:

(1) The conference should be reviewed as organizationally consistent with previous IFCO policy. (As they relate to community organizing both in the procedures for evaluating and funding proposals and of membership on the board.)

(2) IFCO encourages the conference steering committee to become as responsive as possible to the total black community.

(3) IFCO supports the programmatic aspects of the Manifesto and the other conference resolutions.

(4) It is suggested that no IFCO staff member serve on the conference steering committee.

(5) IFCO urges the churches to come up with the basic money to launch the activities of the conference steering committee. This would be approximately:

$195,000 for field staff subsistence for one year.
$ 30,000 for developing the United Black Appeal.
$ 20,000 for printing.
$ 25,000 for travel.

(6) IFCO relinquished its own plans to develop a United Black Appeal in recognition of the plans of the conference to develop such an appeal.

(7) All money to be channeled through IFCO for the conference must be money above and beyond the present church commitments to IFCO. No money which is not specifically designated for the conference will be channeled to it.

The conference, however, should be considered a priority for IFCO in the context of economic development.

In my judgment the introduction of the concept of reparations through the National Black Economic Development Conference occasioned a new level of awareness and an encouraging turn in developments within the movement of black liberation. In the years ahead, our society will need to deal with the question of restitution for its maintenance of and participation in the slave economy and in a dual system that has deprived and denied black citizens equal rights in American society. The guilt of white America has never been expiated in any formal manner. The concept of reparations will allow an opportunity for formal restitution which will not only contribute to the economic development of the black community, but the psychological relief of the white community that can potentially diffuse the rising tension between the races and put us on the road towards viable reform rather than the present tack that we seem to be following towards revolution and conflict in American society.

APPENDIX 4

A Policy Statement by the Synagogue Council of America and the National Jewish Community Relations Advisory Council*

PUBLIC ATTENTION has been focused on the disruption of religious services by spokesmen for a newly created Black Economic Development Conference. The threat that such disruptions and the demands made by the conference will be repeated and enlarged leads the Synagogue Council of America and the National Jewish Community Relations Advisory Council to issue the following statement for the consideration and guidance of synagogues and other Jewish communal institutions.

The "Black Manifesto" issued by the Black Economic Development Conference proposes:

To disrupt divine worship services in churches and synagogues and "the total disruption of selected church-sponsored agencies."

To seize churches and synagogues and hold them in

* The adoption of this statement was reported on May 12, 1969. The Synagogue Council of America is composed of the following: Rabbinical Assembly, Rabbinical Council of America, Central Conference of American Rabbis, United Synagogue of America, Union of Orthodox Jewish Congregations of America, and Union of American Hebrew Congregations. The National Jewish Community Relations Advisory Council is made up of these groups: American Jewish Committee, American Jewish Congress, B'nai B'rith—Anti-Defamation League, Jewish Labor Committee, Jewish War Veterans of the U.S.A., Union of Hebrew Congregations, Union of Orthodox Jewish Congregations of America and United Synagogue of America.

ransom for half a billion dollars "reparations" for 200
years of slavery.
To seize "office telephones and printing apparatus of all
church-related agencies and to hold these in trusteeship until our demands are met."
To resort to violence and force, if necessary, to achieve
these goals.

Two separate issues have been raised by the "Black Manifesto": one by the substance of the demands, the other by the
tactics employed to advance them. We find the demands and
the tactics objectionable on both moral and practical grounds.

(1) The Demands

It is evident that much remains to be done if the racial discrimination that has shamed our American past is to be wiped
out. We believe that it is entirely in order for our religious and
communal institutions—no less than other segments of our
society—to be challenged, both from within and from without,
to face up to their own shortcomings and responsibilities. The
gap between principle and performance is lamentably large;
we have fallen short of our responsibilities in working for
racial and economic justice.

We submit, on the other hand, that the demands for reparations by the Black Economic Development Conference is not
an answer to the inequities and injustices of our society. It is
clear that even if these demands were met in full, these
inequities and injustices would not be rectified. To that end,
a far more reliable guide for priorities is to be found in the
Kerner Commission Report, the "Freedom Budget" of the
A. Philip Randolph Institute and in the National Urban
League's "Domestic Marshall Plan."

What is required is massive government action in the areas
of employment, housing, education, health and welfare. To
say this is not to shirk personal or organizational responsibility,
for such action can come about only if we as citizens declare
and press our determination to pay the substantial costs that
are involved. It is for this reason that the Synagogue Council

of America and the NJCRAC urged their constituents to support the Kerner Commission's far-reaching recommendations and to make known to congressmen their support of the taxes that will be necessary to finance the crucial measures advocated by the commission.

We recognize that developments in the intervening months, including congressional cut-backs of funds for a whole range of domestic programs dealing with poverty and the urban crisis, are hardly calculated to inspire confidence in the seriousness of the national commitment and in the social effectiveness of religious and communal institutions. This is all the more reason why we must not permit public attention to be diverted by misguided demands from the real tasks and challenges that must occupy our energies and commitments.

We therefore urge congregations and communal institutions to:

> Redouble their efforts to effect restorations of state and federal budget cuts in the areas indicated above (i.e., employment, housing, education, health and welfare) and indicate their support of higher taxes, if necessary, adequately to finance these measures.

> Strengthen communication with local black communities, both on the clergy and lay levels, and to contribute to the support of indigenous self-help projects.

The Synagogue Council of America, through its newly established division of urban affairs, the National Jewish Community Relations Advisory Council and their national constituent agencies are prepared to assist synagogues and communal institutions in the implementation of these goals.

(2) *The Tactics*

The tactics resorted to by spokesmen for the Black Economic Development Conference in advancing their demands must also receive our serious attention, for these tactics involve disruption of divine services, demands for "ransom," and threats of violence.

We recognize that Americans "can no longer speak of 'violence' and 'extremism' without the terrible knowledge that their most destructive manifestation in American life is to be found in the violence done to the lives, the hopes and aspirations of our Negro citizens" (SCA policy statement March 6, 1968). It is equally true, however, that even in pursuit of desirable ends, violence does not contribute to the fashioning of a better society; violence only breeds more violence and nourishes repression, not justice.

We further express our conviction that the values by which men's actions and goals are judged are not subject to the exigencies of time and certainly not to those of race. The "revolution" in our cities and on our campuses does not create its own morality. The exegesis which enables some religious leaders to suspend biblical injunctions against violence, arson and murder and to invest these with a special grace when committed in the name of the "revolution" has no sanction in Jewish tradition.

If we speak up at this time, it is not only to clarify our position in regard to the demands and the tactics of the Black Economic Development Conference, but to urge that reprehensible actions not be permitted to divert our attention from the hard tasks which require our efforts and resources if our moral and religious professions are to be taken seriously. By implementing the specific actions outlined above, synagogues and communal institutions will give tangible expression of their commitment to the elimination of the poverty, degradation and hopelessness that still afflict the lives of so many of our fellow citizens.

BEDC Demands Presented to the Roman Catholic Archdiocese of New York

May 9, 1969

To: Cardinal Cooke
From: James Forman
        Director, United Black Appeal
Re: Black Manifesto

The following are facts relating to demands made of the Catholic Church Archdiocese of New York:

(1) "Every year religious organizations gather about $5 billion in contributions. The value of their 'visible assets' has been estimated at $79.5 billion—almost double the combined assets of the country's five largest industrial corporations.

(2) "Of this treasure, approximately $44.5 billion worth is held by the Roman Catholic Church.

(3) "The Catholic Church must be the biggest corporation in the United States. They have a branch office in almost every neighborhood. Their assets and real estate holdings must exceed those of Standard Oil, AT & T, and U.S. Steel combined. Their roster of dues-paying members must be second only to the tax rolls of the U. S. government" (above information taken from *The Religion Business,* by Alfred Balk, page 8, John Knox Press).

(4) "When one remembers that churches pay no inheritance tax (churches do not die), that churches may own and operate

business and be exempt from the 52 percent corporate income tax, and that real property used for church purposes (which in most states are most generally construed) is tax exempt, it is not unreasonable to prophesy that with reasonably prudent management, the churches ought to be able to control the whole economy of the nation within the predictable future"— Doctor Eugene Carson Blake.

We demand a list of all Catholic Church assets, unrelated business income, stock and real-estate investments, pensions, retirements and investment funds. We have demanded 60 percent of profits of all assets from other religious denominations. The percentage demanded from the Catholic Church will be negotiated upon receipt of the list of all assets.

We ask $200 million dollars to establish a southern land bank, as outlined in the Black Manifesto.

We demand that the Catholic Church in America support the Black Manifesto of the National Black Economic Development Conference. The Catholic Church is to use its influence to pressure all white racist Christian churches and Jewish synagogues to meet the demands of the National Black Economic Development Conference for reparations due to the role of the Christian and Jewish religions in exploiting black people in this country.

Response of the Archdiocese,
May 21, 1969

THE RECENT PUBLIC STATEMENTS by Mr. James Forman of the National Black Economic Development Conference have caused all of us to reflect deeply upon some of the frustrations and aspirations of the black people. It is regrettable that in the "Black Manifesto" these concerns are closely joined to political concepts which are completely contrary to our American way of life. On this basis, in addition to the manner of presentation and other substantive considerations, we do not endorse the "Black Manifesto" or its demands.

The people of the Archdiocese of New York have always had, and will ever continue to have, a deep and practical concern for the needy, the disadvantaged, and all who are unjustly deprived because of racial prejudice. This concern is twofold: to provide services to alleviate suffering and to work for the renewal of society in order to remove the root cause of suffering. Such renewal, within the legal framework of our society, must seek to provide equal opportunity for all and should recognize the new spirit of identity and pride within the black community. At the same time, we must learn from the past that every present excess will inevitably aggravate the future.

The Church's concern for the poor is practical. Catholic Charities, through its 203 social welfare agencies, provides a variety of services to the needy and disadvantaged, regardless of race or religion. These services, related to health, family welfare, child care, and youth activities, involved last year a cash expenditure of $5,764,000 donated by the people of the Archdiocese of New York.

In addition, adult education, job opportunity, and housing programs are conducted by the archdiocese on behalf of all the disadvantaged. The parochial school system is preparing children in all neighborhoods to take a meaningful and productive role in society. In areas where the local parishes cannot support these operations, the archdiocese as a whole is providing that support.

Last year the amount spent by the archdiocese to meet the deficit for the cost of the education of inner-city children was $1,279,000. This figure was added to all the direct expenditures of local parishes and individuals.

It is hoped that these voluntary offerings will increase with each passing day. At the same time, it must be recognized that the people of the Archdiocese of New York experience inevitable limitations in what they are able to do from their own resources.

"Reparations" and "collective guilt" are highly controversial concepts. Nevertheless, it is clear that a good society has the responsibility to develop equitable and adequate political, social, and economic opportunities for all its people. In the light of history, there is a particular responsibility toward the black people. In this area, the Church has made persevering efforts to form consciences, to change attitudes and to promote effective legislation. Much more remains to be done; we shall continue to work with all Church members toward the achievement of these ends.

The Church's deep concern stems from the very heart of the message of Jesus, most recently reaffirmed in the words of the Second Vatican Council: "the right to have a share of earthly goods sufficient for oneself and one's family belongs to everyone" (*Pastoral Constitution on Church in Modern World*, n. 69).

The struggle to achieve social justice for all our brothers of all races will continue to challenge our best efforts. No one can feel that enough has been done or that enough is now being done. Now, dynamic, imaginative paths must be sought out and explored. Every proposal—however different and unusual—must be given a full hearing in the hope that it will shed some light on this most urgent of problems.

The Archdiocese of New York will continue to make every possible effort to secure social justice and true equity for all men. The archdiocese will continue to work for all the poor and disadvantaged through its parishes and schools, its adult education, job opportunity and housing programs, through the social welfare agencies of Catholic Charities, through its social justice efforts, and through its established policy of cooperation with other religious and civic groups.

APPENDIX 6

White Churchmen Have a Problem*

Dr. Arthur Flemming
President, National Council of Churches
Macalester College
St. Paul, Minnesota

Dear Dr. Flemming,
White churchmen have a problem. They have been confronted by an adversary whom they choose not to recognize but whose message wrecks havoc with their consciences. They would like to walk both sides of the fence. That is, for the sake of the body of white constituents they will not speak of recognition, while, in hopes of pacifying black churchmen, they would encourage us to sit with them in consultations with the National Black Economic Development Conference. We refuse to be used in this way.

We must remind you that in the course of searching for a response, white churchmen persistently voiced the plea that they be advised by black churchmen as to what they ought to do. Black churchmen have not ignored this plea. At every turn we have spoken to you on this point. We have spoken independently; we have spoken through many of the several black caucuses; and, finally, we have spoken through the

---

* This statement to the president of the National Council of Churches was made by an ad hoc group of the National Committee of Black Churchmen (NCBC) on June 26, three days after the executive committee of the Council voted to "consult" with NBEDC leaders through a special sixteen-man committee to include NCBC delegates. The NCBC is an ecumenical organization made up of black caucuses in Protestant denominations and the Roman Catholic Church.

powerful instrumentality of the National Committee of Black Churchmen. In each of these instances our message has been simple and unambiguous. We have advised white churchmen formally to recognize the NBEDC. At the June 23, 1969 meeting of the Executive Committee of the National Council of Churches, white churchmen, with cold deliberateness, refused to vote recognition of the NBEDC. Another element of our advice was, and is, that you demonstrate that recognition by voting to urge the denominations to provide a minimum of $270,000 through IFCO to NBEDC for the purpose of getting the initial administrative and field services needs of NBEDC off the ground. You white churchmen did not even consider this matter.

In view of the foregoing, and in light of the fact that we recognize your demonstrated indifference to our opinions as a totally unacceptable insult, we advise you that no black churchmen shall sit with either eight or eighty of you to discuss anything with the NBEDC. You have chosen to make NBEDC a problem. We will not be party to that problem, nor are we disposed to be, or to appear to be, aligned with you and your negativeness in any consultations which you may, as you indeed ought to, have with the NBEDC.

Unmistakably, our position is one of recognition of and support for NBEDC. You have rejected this position out of hand. In so doing, we are constrained to communicate to you our strongly held belief that you have chosen to reject us. This is not a problem for us, because that is inherently the norm in our racist society. It is a tragedy for the church, because we live in a day in which turmoil and tension offer opportunities never before seen, but you have failed to open the door to the opportunity to give black churchmen equal respect with yourselves.

The door is not necessarily closed for good. You still have the option and the power to open it. The keys to such a beginning must take the form of a formal recognition of the NBEDC by you, and the body over which you preside, and a formal urging of the denominations to provide $270,000. Until that has been accomplished, you must know that we are of one mind in our determination that we shall not be used.

APPENDIX 7

A Reparations Jubilee

by the Editors of World Outlook*

THERE ARE many aspects of the current demand of militant blacks for "reparations" from the churches that seem calculated to make the blood boil in most whites and even in many church-going Negroes. Few churchmen relish the thought of interrupted worship services, liberals don't enjoy hearing a famous liberal church such as Riverside in New York called a "racist institution," and no one likes the thought of intimidation and threats to "disrupt" selected churches and synagogues. Most Americans, in church or out, don't agree that the capitalist system is "the most vicious, racist system in the world." In short, Mr. James Forman's language was not learned in a Dale Carnegie course on How to Win Friends and Influence People.

And there are deeper problems than that of language. The general public wonders who Mr. Forman is and what is the nature of the projects for which he demands five hundred million dollars? What are the possibilities that a "white backlash" as a result of these tactics will undo much of the work and achievements of progressive—but not revolutionary—civil rights organizations? How does one decide which groups receive reparations—if blacks, why not American Indians, and if they, why not Mexican Americans, and if they . . . ? And which churches should pay and on what basis? Et cetera, et cetera, et cetera. The mind boggles.

* This editorial statement appeared in the June 1969 issue of *World Outlook,* published by the Board of Missions of the United Methodist Church, New York. It is used by permission.

Supporters of the Manifesto would reply by pointing out that our society demands such tactics and language. Who would ever have paid any attention to Mr. Forman if he had genteelly distributed the document on the streets outside Riverside Church? Who would have paid attention to the Manifesto itself if it had meekly suggested certain reforms? Mr. Forman himself is no latecomer to the scene, and the Manifesto does spell out a concrete program, a program which tends to get overlooked in the struggle over tactics.

In addition, there are, as Riverside's pastor Doctor Ernest T. Campbell said, "sound theological underpinnings" to the principle of reparations. We're not sure what underpinnings Doctor Campbell had in mind, but to us it is clear that if a church confesses its sins in the matter of race it should do what it can to make restitution. If we come before the altar to confess before God, and then remember that we have sinned against our brother, the Gospel is clear that we should first go and be reconciled with our brother.

Experience affirms what the Bible proclaims—the sins of the fathers do have a way of being visited on the children to the third and fourth generation. No generation—either of the much sinning or the much sinned against—starts with a clean slate. And anyone who believes that restitution is made by mere verbal confession or without pain has understood neither the force of Jesus' parables nor the atonement itself. Jesus did not tell people to "kiss and make up," but "Go, sell what you have and give to the poor." The reconciliation taught by Christ in both word and example was nothing if not painful.

Now in our situation, if we cut through the revolutionary rhetoric of the Black Manifesto (which isn't easy to do), it is clear that the churches have not begun to repent of their complicity in slavery, in the enslavement of the black man. "They came in chains" with the approval and support of the Church of Jesus Christ. Money will no more atone for that than it will for napalm on Vietnamese children—but it will be a visible and concrete sign of repentance. The only thing surprising about the call for reparations is that no one thought of it sooner. Despite the complicated practical questions, the basic principle is Gospel clear.

Fundamentally, reparations is a scheme for the rearrangement of wealth to offset past inequities or correct an imbalance in society. The ancient Israelites had such a scheme, though it wasn't called reparations. Every seven years (the "Sabbatical") and later every fifty years (the "Jubilee Year," Leviticus 25) the land would lie fallow, debts suspended (or usury ended), Hebrew slaves emancipated, and certain property which had been sold redeemed. The proposal recognized that in a society where some people are more acquisitive than others, social conditions can go astray. The religious principle —which is not altogether compatible with capitalism—was that the land as well as the people should keep the Sabbath to God for, after all, the land really belonged to God. All Israelites are God's servants and, therefore, cannot be permanently owned by other Hebrews. Scholars say the utopian Jubilee Year never worked, but it and the Sabbatical are reminders that we are all no more than stewards of our possessions and, as a society, periodically in need of rejuggling.

It was this kind of social redistribution that our Lord may have had in mind—if we take him literally—when he announced in his home town that Scripture had been fulfilled and that we would celebrate a kind of Jubilee with Him.

"The Spirit of the Lord is upon me, because he has anointed me to preach good news to the poor. He has sent me to proclaim release to the captives and recovering of sight to the blind, to set at liberty those who are oppressed, to proclaim the acceptable year of the Lord."

These days, the Bible seems to turn up only "hard sayings." Perhaps this is God's way of reminding us that the Gospel makes radical claims upon us. If we approach the questions of reparations in this sense, Mr. Forman and the Black Manifesto have done us all a service. The specific programs, the violent rhetoric, the revolutionary tactics—all of these are open to discussion. After all, the framers of this Manifesto are as much under the judgment of God as any of the rest of us. But let us not presume to know that judgment before we search our own corporate lives. For our screams of rage may be only the pain resulting from the exposure of a moral nerve.

APPENDIX 8

"I Hear My Brother"

by Religious News Service (6-20-69)*

PHILADELPHIA (RNS). A member of the National Black Economic Development Conference, which is seeking $500 million in "reparations" from the nation's churches and synagogues, was "moved" to speak at a Quaker service at a Friends' meeting house here.

Muhammed Kenyatta, twenty-five, of Chester, Pa., who represents NBEDC in the Greater Philadelphia area, held the "flag of the American black people" as he addressed participants in the 6th Annual National Workshop on Christian Unity, which concluded a five-day session here.

Mr. Kenyatta sought to speak early in the service, but Francis Browne, general secretary of the Philadelphia yearly meeting, who was describing the new meeting house to workshop delegates, asked him to wait.

As worship began, there was prolonged silence dotted with a few brief prayers; then Mr. Kenyatta rose to speak. Reverently, he said, "Our witness is not to an abstract God. Our witness should be to flesh and blood. We feel moved to say as Gandhi said—that God has no right to appear to the hungry other than as bread."

In a reference to Mr. Browne's remark about Philadelphia being the birthplace of liberty, Mr. Kenyatta, who formerly had a storefront Baptist church in North Philadelphia, said, "That's a sacrilege to my people. To us this is the burial place

* This news account reflects many aspects of the serious, emotional feeling which accompanied the Manifesto. It is reprinted by permission of Religious News Service, June 20, 1969.

of the Indian nation. We have lost love or historical respect for anyone—Quaker, Jew, Episcopal, Roman Catholic—whose history is with those who helped con the Indians out of what was theirs."

Mr. Browne rose to ask Kenyatta to conclude his remarks—"so we can continue with worship."

Mr. Kenyatta replied, "I am worshipping."

There was a loud chorus of "amen" from the audience in support of Mr. Kenyatta when Sister Mary Simon of the Holy Child Order arose and said, "I hear my brother. His words are right and true. I ask that we listen to him."

Then Mr. Kenyatta explained that he was addressing the unity workshop because "any unity of the Christian Churches is a unification of white racism. It's a step toward white nationalism. We speak to the church universal when we speak for the peasant who makes movement of the Rosary in Peru while the Catholic Church reaps a fortune greater than that of General Motors," said Mr. Kenyatta.

He said, "We are just calling for a concrete expression of our Christian love."

"I used to love other people (apparently white people)," he said, "And I hope someday I can again. But I can't love them now; I can't love those who now misuse me."

Mr. Browne rose again and asked that the worship be concluded and the rest of Kenyatta's remarks be considered part of a business meeting.

Mr. Kenyatta took that opportunity to say that the switch from worship to business symbolized "a problem we have with the churches—they always have to distinguish between secular and religious."

"For too long," he charged, "we have been taught at gunpoint and by whiplash to lay down at the feet, not of Jesus, but of white Americans."

The principle behind the Black Manifesto, which is being promulgated by the NBEDC, he said, is the same as that behind the Jews receiving reparations from Germany "for the unspeakable massacre of their people."

"Think of 'reparations' as a chance to repair and restore," Mr. Kenyatta concluded.

Chronology

THE FOLLOWING CHRONOLOGY related to the Black Manifesto is far
from exhaustive in terms of pro and con stances voiced by churchmen and other public figures. Nor can it contain the hundreds of
opinions from local religious and civil rights groups. In these respects it can only reflect the variety. Neither are all local Manifesto
events recorded. The listing concentrates on happenings taken to
be the most significant during the first early months of the National
Black Economic Development Conference. A few dates prior to the
Manifesto's appearance are given to show the magnitude of the
American racial-economic crisis, and to illustrate the heightening
importance of the economic factors in projected solutions. If persons involved in a development note a date a day or so later than
a decision was made, it is because actions and reports often do not
coincide. The editors have made every effort to be completely
accurate. Abbreviations for organizations are used only on second
reference and thereafter.

September, 1967
> Interreligious Foundation for Community Organization (IFCO)
> begins work.

March, 1968
> National Advisory Commission on Civil Disorders (Kerner
> Commission) tells U.S. "white racism" is major cause of urban
> problems.

April 4, 1968
> Assassination of Martin Luther King, Jr.; along with Kerner
> Report spurs most religious groups to greater planning and

spending to aid minorities, pledges reach near $50 million by Fall, some millions spent.

Summer, 1968
King-planned Poor People's Campaign in Washington, D.C., thrusts jobs, housing, education and medical needs of poor before government and people; no significant public action.

September, 1968
IFCO launches plans for a National Black Economic Development Conference (NBEDC) in early 1969.

October, 1968
National Committee of Black Churchmen (NCBC) holds national convocation; new militancy and disappointment with white religious establishment heard along with calls for black control of white funded community development and organizational projects.

November, 1968–January, 1969
Period of national waiting as Nixon Administration shapes up.

(*all dates following are 1969*)
March
Urban America—Urban Coalition reports no change in attacking roots of racism since Kerner Report.

April 4
First anniversary of King murder; second stage of Poor People's Campaign stresses increased direct public aid to the poor.

Mid-April
Concern of some U.S. senators over poverty stirs mixed reactions; skepticism about Nixon's "black capitalism" voiced by blacks.

April 25–27
NBEDC meets in Detroit.

April 26
Black Manifesto passed by vote of 187 to 63 out of some 500 participants, no rescinding action taken; idea of reparations injected into race issue; NBEDC set to continue as organization, tentative steering committee named.

May 1
James Forman presents Manifesto to Episcopal Church leaders in New York.

Lucius Walker, IFCO director, addresses National Council of Churches (NCC) General Board, explains seriousness of points made at Detroit meeting.

May 2

Forman presents Manifesto to NCC board, referred to 33 constituent Protestant and Orthodox churches, and NCC executive secretary R. H. Edwin Espy to report to executive committee on June 23.

May 3

Forman meets with Ernest Campbell of Riverside Church, New York; informal agreement for Manifesto to be distributed outside church next day in lieu of public reading later reported by Campbell.

May 4

Riverside worship interrupted by Forman; specific demands to congregation made, Campbell and two-thirds of worshippers walk out.

Picketing of churches in Detroit postponed because of NCC referral of Manifesto to churches.

May 5

Reaction to Riverside incident mixed, church leaders cautious; New York Mayor John Lindsay tells churches to alert police to disruptions; Lindsay and Campbell criticized by some black churchmen; civil rights advocate Bayard Rustin scores Forman.

Principle of reparations endorsed by ad hoc black caucus formed by 35 national black churchmen. They say black as well as white must increase role in development and moves toward social justice.

May 6

Forman posts demands, including $50 million for NBEDC work, on door of New York headquarters of Lutheran Church in America, hands copy to LCA president Robert Marshall.

IFCO board meets to consider future relation to NBEDC, caucus of white and black members first convene, IFCO president Rabbi Marc Tanenbaum against endorsing Manifesto; board sees NBEDC as independent unit, pledges to help it get going, turns over plan for United Black Appeal, backs program aspects, suggests IFCO staff not serve on NBEDC committee.

May 7

Directors of NCBC hear Forman in Atlanta, support Manifesto in principle; NCBC executive Metz Rollins instructed to help coordinate support.

May 8

Baltimore Catholic archdiocesan paper calls Forman a "stunt man."

May 9

Forman and Rollins present demands for $200 million from American Catholicism to New York Archdiocese; Terence Cardinal Cooke away.

Forman gets restraining order from Riverside against worship interruptions; he burns it.

Kenneth G. Neigh, general secretary of United Presbyterian Board of National Missions, IFCO member, sends letter to all pastors of Church rejecting rhetoric and tactics of NBEDC, regrets IFCO link to Manifesto.

Falsely rumored that Forman will appear at New York's Temple Emanu-El during worship, members of Jewish Defense League surround area, Rabbi Nathan Perilman deplores league action.

Forman appears on "Night Call," national call-in radio program, underscores view that members—especially rich trustees—of churches and synagogues are being asked for funds as well as national agencies.

May 10

Campbell announces Riverside's response; reparations endorsed, funds scoped for minority development but none for NBEDC.

Harlem's *Amsterdam News* editorially criticizes Forman tactics.

May 11

Forman revisits Riverside, no NBEDC interruptions; shares press conference with Campbell and hits white-launched alternatives to NBEDC.

Ten NBEDC supporters arrested outside First United Methodist Church, Los Angeles, after reading Manifesto inside; charges dropped two days later, bond posted by local clergy.

May 12

Synagogue Council of America and National Jewish Community Relations Advisory Council—collectively representing most U.S. Jewish groups—report rejection of "substance" and "tactics" of Manifesto, call for other approaches for solving racial and economic problems.

Black and white students at New York's Union Theological Seminary seize building, demanding school and its directors give heavily to NBEDC.

May 13

Specific demands, including $60 million for IFCO, presented by Forman and Rollins to Episcopal presiding Bishop John E. Hines.

Union Seminary occupation ends when directors set special meeting.

Ralph Abernathy, King's successor, takes Poor People's Campaign to White House in meeting with Nixon and President's Urban Affairs Council, calls session "friendly" but "fruitless."

May 14

NBEDC supporters occupy Neigh's office in New York's Interchurch Center, list demands for blacks and Spanish-Americans; United Presbyterian General Assembly opening in San Antonio; Forman invited to speak.

Uneasiness over IFCO tie to NBEDC heard in Protestant quarters.

Walker of IFCO responds to charges by Los Angeles policeman that agency gave large sums to "militant and disruptive" groups, denies direct grants to Black Panthers; reports say policeman's data turned over to federal agency; Walker denies IFCO secrecy.

James Lawson, chairman of Black Methodist for Church Renewal, says reparation is serious proposal for constructive work.

Forman hands demands, including $130 million for black university and $10 million for Black Appeal, to president Ben Mohr Herbster of United Church of Christ (UCC) and Howard Spragg of United Board for Homeland Ministries, suggests university at UCC-related Tougaloo College, Miss.; incident not reported until June 3.

May 15

Additional space "liberated" in United Presbyterian mission offices.

Union seminary directors approve capital and funds from drive for black development, none for NBEDC; sums to be administered by black faculty, students, directors and alumni.

Forman addresses United Presbyterian Assembly, asks $80 million for IFCO; spokesmen for Spanish-Americans also make demands.

May 16

Special committee named by United Presbyterian moderator to bring recommendations on demands.

Black Methodists for Church Renewal (BMCR) urge denominational support for reparations; name representatives to NBEDC steering committee.

Episcopal Bishop Roger Blanchard of southern Ohio refuses to accept or endorse Manifesto.

May 17

Walker addresses American Baptist Convention (ABC) in Seattle, defends IFCO.

Forman gives demands, including $60 million for IFCO, to ABC; reparation backed by Samuel B. McKinney, leader of Black American Baptist Churchmen, principle said to have some merit by Thomas Kilgore, Jr., new ABC president and a black.

May 18

Herman Holmes of NBEDC hands John Cardinal Cody of Chicago the Manifesto during a Mass; archdiocese asked for $5 to $7 million, no response told.

Union of Orthodox Jewish Congregations call for national legislature to protect worship from disruption.

May 19

United Presbyterian Assembly votes at least $50 million drive for "depressed areas and depressed people," $100,000 for IFCO, land and funds for Spanish-American programs, other development action.

May 19–26

World Council of Churches Consultation on Church and Racism in London; reparation becomes major issue; NBEDC group interrupts with demand of about $70 million, "to redress the balance of power against oppressed people"; request seen as aimed at 235 constituent Protestant and Orthodox WCC members; Channing Phillips, first black to receive presidential nomination at U.S. political convention, backs reparations, delegate from South Africa says idea given up there; meeting asks WCC to back reparations and revolution as "last resort" in fight against racism, proposals go to WCC Central Committee for consideration.

May 20

Hines of Episcopal Church hits language and philosophy of Manifesto but asks executive council to respond.

May 21

Roman Catholic Archdiocese of New York rejects demands, says Manifesto causes deep reflection on "some of the frustrations and aspirations of the black people"; charity and educational programs cited.

Episcopal executive council rejects demands, cites a total of $13 million since 1967, states need to fight poverty, sets committee; Quintin Primo of Episcopal Union of Black Clergy and Laymen not pleased with response.

Riverside church meeting on Manifesto, task force to study congregation's percentage to development told.

United Presbyterian Assembly adopts statement to be read in all churches on May 25, sees black and Spanish spokesmen as God-sent; Manifesto itself found to contain much to be "unalterably opposed."

Christian Century magazine disagrees with those calling reparation ridiculous but sees problems in effective implementation, warns against civil rights and civil liberties becoming enemies.

May 22

Rollins of NCBC calls response of New York Catholic Archdiocese an "almost absolute affront to the black church"; Father Lawrence Lucas of Harlem sees it as "dishonest."

Take-over of Presbyterian offices ends; another group holds four United Methodist mission board floors in Interchurch Center for eight hours; leader is Cain Felder, director of BMCR; mission board agrees to special meeting on demands for more than one billion, including $750,000 for NBEDC.

NBEDC asks Church Federation of Chicago for $30,000; demand turned over to a committee.

Board of Christian Education of Presbyterian Church, U.S., (southern) says church members should listen honestly to Manifesto message; no rejection or approval given.

Bobby Brown of Black United Youth of Little Rock reported to plan Manifesto drive in Arkansas; church leaders react philosophically.

Michigan Christian Advocate (United Methodist) asks churches not to call police if interrupted, hopes Manifesto will wake up people but sees NBEDC as potentially harmful.

May 23

Newspaper of Catholic Diocese of Worcester, Mass., finds religion has done little for blacks but sees Manifesto in terms of the "protection racket."

Rabbi Irving Lehmann, vice-president of Synagogue Council of America, tells Miami Beach congregation neither uncritical capitulation or flat rejection of black demands is good, urges reassessment of commitment to poor and afflicted.

Catholic Archbishop Karl Alter of Cincinnati rejects Manifesto as "intemperate" in letter to clergy.

Mrs. Martin Luther King, Jr., calls reparations "equitable symbolism" but rejects idea in favor of mass church pressure on U.S. Congress; she addresses joint Catholic Press Association-Associated Church Press meeting in Atlanta.

May 24

Church press groups vote to help readers reach "informed, responsible" response to Manifesto.

Ava Maria, Catholic magazine, sees issues Manifesto raises looming with "nightmare urgency" before religious leaders, hopes for solutions apart from pressure groups.

May 25

Series of walk-ins to read Manifesto begins by Black Radical Action Project in Indianapolis.

Black Liberation Front walks into Second Presbyterian Church, St. Louis, to read demands for $50 million from area Presbyterians; first of the "Black Sundays" conducted by the Front and ACTION.

May 26

NBEDC steering committee votes to enlarge to include more

churchmen; Walker chairs session, then bows out of future active participation.

United Methodist mission board executive committee rejects demand to give to NBEDC, offers $1.3 million for black development to be administered by black staff and black bishops; offer rejected by Felder; black Bishop Charles Golden takes dim view of administration proposal.

Christianity and Crisis magazine says prime debate must be on principle of reparation, with "how" coming second; finds Manifesto requiring churches to decide whose side they are on.

May 27

General Board of Christian Church (Disciples of Christ) declines to give "yes" or "no" to reparations; Manifesto labeled "black racism," but call made for radical change in attitude on race crisis in church.

Eugene Carson Blake, WCC head, says Manifesto is indication that challenge to "even the most progressive free enterprise is sharper today than before," refuses to lead revolutionaries out of church, asks response take laymen into account.

Gallup Poll, surveying 1,515 adults between May 23–27, finds two percent of whites and 21 percent of black populations supporting reparations; 27 percent of blacks undecided.

May 28

J. H. Jackson, president of National Baptist Convention, U.S.A., Inc., nation's largest black denomination, scores Manifesto as "totalitarian."

Request of coalition of 30 Mexican-American groups in Bay Area for $350,000 from Catholic Archdiocese of San Francisco reported; unofficial response says canvas of all members necessary before such a grant could be made.

May 29

Missouri West United Methodist Conference votes $450,000 to $550,000 in capital funds to Black Methodists for Church Renewal.

May 30

Commonweal, Catholic magazine, finds "little of controversy" in program aspects of Manifesto; sees language of "insurrection" unfortunate; asks Catholics to do better than the "lack of hospitality" of New York Archdiocese.

May 31

Metropolitan Boston Committee of Black Churchmen ask $100 million for area churches; other specific demands to First and Second Churches of Christ Scientist.

June 1

St. Louis reparation supporters allowed to read demands at Memorial Presbyterian Church, turned away at Ascension Catholic; churches seek legal recourse.

Service interrupted and Manifesto read in Christ Cranbrook Episcopal Church, Detroit; $100,000 asked.

The Living Church, unofficial Episcopal magazine, urges all to "keep their cool" but asks full review of Church's IFCO tie.

June 2

Blacks make unscheduled presentation of Boston demands to annual meeting of the Mother Church of the Christian Scientists.

President of Methodist Publishing House, Nashville, tells employees of "additional security precautions" because of Manifesto language.

June 3

Demands to United Church of Christ become known; UCC president Herbster reports no response.

June 4

Demands for $20,000 for NBEDC campaign and office space made to Westminster Press (United Presbyterian), Philadelphia; Muhammed Kenyatta, NBEDC steering committee, "borrows" a typewriter; no charges pressed.

June 5

NBEDC takes over offices of Reformed Church in America in Interchurch Center, first "liberation" led by Forman; minimal demands made.

NCC's Division of Christian Life and Mission request member churches not to call police in interruptions unless "dangerous and destructive."

Study group under National Commission on Causes and Prevention of Violence reports Americans have always been violent people "given to a kind of historical amnesia" marking past turbulence, partly because of "our historical vision of ourselves as a latter day chosen people, a new Jerusalem."

June 6

Forman addressed Reformed Church (RCA) General Synod, New Brunswick, N.J.: general secretary says Church will listen but not give in to demands.

NBEDC group temporarily abandons RCA office to seize space of NCC and United Presbyterian mission board; "liberation" ends after agencies agree to study demands; seizures aimed at stepping up attention to NBEDC programs.

Trustees of Interchurch Center consider occupations, no decision to seek restraining order.

Christian Science board of directors makes point-by-point response, rejects $100 million for NBEDC through IFCO, says it cannot disclose financial assets, voices desire to contribute to well-being of black community.

Christianity Today magazine scores religious liberals for "leading on" Forman while they decide "what the church is for"; attribute "whole ridiculous situation" to "repudiation of biblical revelation."

June 7

NBEDC group occupies vacant Redeemer Presbyterian Church, Detroit; Forman asks $50,000 from Presbyterians in area for headquarters; Citizens Against Racism, a white Manifesto support unit, takes over denominaion's Detroit offices.

June 8

Forman speaks from pulpit of New York's St. George Episcopal Church at invitation of rector.

Black Sundays continue in St. Louis; Mass at St. Louis Cathedral interrupted by ACTION, statement says demonstrations may include "spitting into Communion cup"; 75 percent of archdiocesan income asked for urban programs.

June 9

Strike by black and Puerto Rican employees at Interchurch Center called by Forman; estimates of success vary from 20 to 85 percent absenteeism.

Evangelist Billy Graham declines to comment on Manifesto when he arrives in New York for crusade; notes church responsibility in alleviating poverty.

June 10

Report to National Commission on Causes and Prevention of Violence says U.S. will carry out "widespread" political and social reforms or develop into a "society of garrison cities."

Leaders of Disciples Reconciliation crisis fund asks top level national interreligious meeting to deal with "unilateral" demands of Manifesto and responses.

American Church Union, unofficial High Church Episcopal organization, decides to review IFCO membership.

June 11

IFCO board reaffirms May 6 position on NBEDC; Earl E. Allen, a black United Methodist from Houston, succeeds Rabbi Tanenbaum as IFCO president; some report wavering church support for IFCO.

Reformed Church's Synod rejects Forman's ideology, plans and tactics, calls for black caucus in denomination to disburse fund of at least $100,000 for minorities; occupation of offices ends.

NBEDC "liberates" United Church of Christ's Board for Homeland Ministries in Interchurch Center; earlier demands reiterated; office stays virtually closed until end of month.

John Cardinal Carberry of St. Louis declares archdiocese will not condone planned church interruptions or tolerate "blasphemous threats" against the Sacrament of Communion.

(Southern) Baptist Students Concerned, unofficial group calls on denomination's annual convention in New Orleans to understand political and economic situation producing Manifesto and to endorse some programs, such as Southern Land Bank, and back IFCO.

Philadelphia Manifesto-backers occupy Quaker settlement house in Chester.

June 12

Southern Baptist Convention rejects as "outrageous" Manifesto demands, principles and methods.

Forman says demands raised to three billion dollars, additional for black education.

Charles Spivey, Jr., head of NCC's department of social justice, says Manifesto requires churches and synagogues to "put up or shut up" as he appears on NBC's *Huntley-Brinkley Report.*

Christian Advocate, official United Methodist magazine, says Manifesto is one other judgment against the Church for failure to live "for" the world.

Typewriter borrowed from Westminster Press returned.

June 13

NBEDC and Michigan Presbyterian Synod negotiate, demands dropped; Detroit Presbyterian's Black Caucus and NBEDC agree to form coalition to achieve community programs.

NCBC Commission on Theology supports reparations in a statement aiming at theologizing black revolution and a rejection of a Christian outlook identifying Gospel with white formulations.

NCC officials and others "liberated" call on NBEDC to let up on pressure.

Officials of Interchurch Center and agencies occupied decide to legally restrain Forman and NBEDC from take-overs.

Theresa Hoover, associate general secretary of United Methodist mission board, tells missionary conference that Forman has pushed "pseudoreligion" aside and opened the windows.

June 15

Lutheran Witness Reporter, official newspaper of the Lutheran Church Missouri Synod, advises patience with disruptions and serious attention to conditions producing Manifesto; says tactics cannot be condoned.

Three blacks arrested in St. Louis as Black Sundays continue; ACTION reads demands to Episcopal Diocese of Missouri at the Church of the Holy Communion, Universal City.

June 16

Sister Cecilia Goldman, who took part in ACTION interruptions in St. Louis, is said to no longer be a member in "good standing" by Maryknoll Order.

Interchurch Center restraining order against Forman presented, hearing set June 19; Forman ignores it and locks self in UCC office vacated the night before by other liberators.

June 17

NCBC meets in New York and forms Reparations Committee;

Forman attends, also holds press conference in UCC office; Interchurch Center plaintiffs say they are "deeply sympathetic" to causes of poor but cannot tolerate occupations.

Ad Hoc white clergy group in Boston forms to help blacks raise $100 million.

June 18

Association of Boston Urban Priests says it will try to get white churches and synagogues to respond positively to Manifesto; endorses reparations.

American Jewish Committee withdraws from IFCO, mainly because foundation not felt to have clear position on Manifesto; is said a new Jewish coalition may fund through but not belong to IFCO; action not reported until June 30.

Forman attends NCC staff meeting in Interchurch Center; staff objects to restraining order.

June 19

NCC delays Forman court hearing for a week.

NBEDC leaders meet in UCC office not covered by restraining order to warn that blacks in predominantly white churches may pull out over negative Manifesto response; Forman present but does not do talking; one spokesman is Charles Cobb, head of UCC's Committee for Racial Justice Now.

UCC's administrative committee of executive council rejects demands, rhetoric of Manifesto; Cobb accuses his Church of evading the cry of the black community.

Sixth Annual National Workshop on Christian Unity in Philadelphia hears Kenyatta during Quaker-type worship.

June 20

St. Louis Presbyterian rejects Black Liberation Front's demand for $50 million.

Second United Methodist Conference on new and furloughed missionaries asks mission board to place economic development funds under black community control, says Manifesto reminds Church of "how demanding the Gospel of Jesus Christ is."

June 21

Ralph Abernathy and Andrew Young of Southern Christian Leadership Conference wire Espy of NCC, saying the only question to debate on Manifesto is whether the Lord is speaking through it; criticize churches on poor stewardship but no direct endorsement of Manifesto.

June 22

National Association of Laymen (Catholic) say Catholic Church should give $400 million annually instead of $200 million to minority development; does not specify NBEDC.

Directors of Association of Council Secretaries (local church council and NCC executives) urge NCC to reorder priorities to step up positive action to injustices told in Manifesto; also urge NCC "to seek positive alternatives to legal action."

Peaceful demonstrations by black groups in St. Louis; Episcopal Bishop George Cadigan says contributions to poor by church have been "modest."

June 23

Executive committee of NCC agrees to consult with NBEDC through a sixteen-man committee of executives and blacks, including members of NCBC.

Conference on Inner-City Ministry of American Lutheran Church (ALC) asks $14 million of denomination's council, $9 million for NBEDC and $5 million for other minority programs; reparations endorsed by the session, attended by 100, mostly whites.

National board of the unofficial Episcopal Society for Cultural and Racial Unity says reparations are consistent with biblical heritage.

General Board of Church of the Brethren urged by only black member to deal with Manifesto because rhetoric "won't get any better."

June 24

Rollins of NCBC hits NCC executive decision as insufficient, demands recognition of NBEDC.

June 25

NCBC ad hoc group has all day retreat at Interchurch Center; white support group holds a teach-in there.

Forman appears at UCC General Synod in Boston, asks withdrawal of mission agency from restraining order, long debate, withdrawal voted.

American Baptist executive committee rejects ideology and rhetoric of Manifesto but thanks God for "the call to repentance" it represents.

ALC Church Council rejects "strong, coarse, seditious" language of Manifesto, later includes over $4 million in budget for urban and minority work.

Evangelical Covenant Church votes $67,000 yearly until $335,000 raised for black development, administration to involve black covenanters; action comes before annual meeting hears Manifesto explained.

Eight white Episcopal women end sit-in at Bishop Richard Emrich's Detroit office, protesting his refusal to meet officially with NBEDC; he agrees to closed meeting.

June 26

NCBC leaders refuse to take part in NCC special committee to "consult" with NBEDC until Manifesto group officially recognized and churches asked for $270,000 to begin NBEDC administration.

Forman hearing on restraining order postponed at request of his attorneys.

Rabbinical Council of America (Orthodox rabbis) reject reparation, claiming it would polarize white and black America.

June 27

Task Force on Urban Problems, composed of representatives of U.S. Catholic Conference units and Catholic organizations, reported to ask Catholics to listen respectfully to Manifesto and other minority demands.

Council of Secretaries (executives) of United Methodists authorize examination of Manifesto, calls on bishops to set special meeting to consider it.

Catawba Synod (N.C. and Va.; mostly black) of United Presbyterians reject Forman principles as "socialistic" but condone ideals of Manifesto.

Federal investigation of NBEDC reported in Detroit to see if demands constitute extortion or conspiracy for extortion.

Favorable opinion on reparations voiced by Philadelphia-based district of African Methodist Episcopal Church in meeting. Manifesto said to challenge churches to break with past.

June 28

UCC's Churchmen for Racial and Social Justice make demands to General Synod, many programs asked like Manifesto.

Joint meeting of high level church leaders in St. Louis reported; purpose to discuss needs of community arising out of Black Sundays, no common plans immediately told.

Church of the Brethren annual conference establishes unspecified sum as fund to aid minorities.

June 28–29

Pastoral from all top religious leaders read in St. Louis synagogues and churches; racism called "reprehensible," need to hear voices speaking in anguish noted, action urged in seven-point program; reparations and worship disruptions scored.

June 29

Noon Mass at St. Louis Cathedral cancelled when ACTION members refuse to move from communion rail; walk-ins at other area churches.

Father Lawrence Lucas, New York Catholic priest and NBEDC steering committee member, accused Cardinal Cody of "conscious and deliberate racism" in sermon in Chicago.

Barnard Lee, SCLC staff, backs church-paid reparations for alleviating hunger, poor housing and social ills but not for guns; speaks in Philadelphia.

June 30

NCC special committee meets; NCBC and NBEDC boycott, four blacks of member churches attend; proposals discussed include recognition of NBEDC, withdrawal of restraining order and recommendation to supply $270,000 to organize NBEDC; only proposals to be processed in regular way through executive committee, NCC General Board, and passed to communions.

UCC votes Commission on Racial Justice with majority of black members; grants funds for operation, votes feasibility studies on supporting black university, southern land bank, black publishing and printing—proposals found in Manifesto.

African Methodist Episcopal Zion Bishop Stephen Spottswood, chairman of NAACP directors, raps reparations and NBEDC, says some white leaders gullible.

Action of United Methodist Rocky Mountain Conference reported, rejecting reparations but setting asistance to minorities and asking Board of Missions to keep channels to NBEDC open and make alternate proposals.

July 1

Rally in Detroit protests federal investigation of NBEDC.

Moderator R. Matthew Lynn and the Council on Church and Society of the Presbyterian Church, U.S., say neither uncritical endorsement nor outright rejection of Manifesto proper; reparation seen as helpful word for the Church; reexamination of denominational programs asked.

J. Lem Stokes II, executive head of United Methodist Quadrennial Emphasis Committee, says Manifesto both causing backlash against Church's $20 million Fund for Reconciliation and causing greater interest in what church ought to do to establish justice.

July 2

Protests to federal investigation in Detroit, Boston, New York and Philadelphia; Robert E. Morrison, white Detroit Episcopal priest, refused to testify before grand jury.

Milton Henry, officer of separatist Republic of New Africa, calls NBEDC, "counterrevolutionary idiocy"; wants reparations for his organization.

Lawson of black Methodist caucus asks for 70 percent of $20 million reconciliation fund for black agencies; $180,000 later voted for black caucus, and large grants go to minority organization; Lawson says pressure within Church to fire Cain Felder, director of caucus, because of support of NBEDC.

Plans for a national conference of church leaders and blacks told by United Black Churchmen of United Church of Christ; NCC asked to launch.

July 3

Philadelphia NBEDC takes over Cookman United Methodist Church, asking that it be turned over for community use; church mainly white.

July 5

40 Catholics of Archdiocese of Los Angeles go to Fresno to present demand for $10 million annually for minorities to Los

Angeles Coadjutor Archbishop-designate Timothy Manning; bishop not in; moratorium on church building urged.

July 6

Washington Square United Methodist church, New York, gives Forman and NBEDC $15,000 during morning worship; first contribution from predominantly white church.

Black Sunday leads to violence in St. Louis Cathedral; three blacks arrested, members of congregation try to attack disrupters; later, Cardinal Carberry and cathedral pastor ask injunction against disturbances; archdiocese denies ownership of slum property, allegation made by ACTION and Black Liberation Front; newspaper investigation supports archdiocese's claim.

No service at Philadelphia's Cookman church; take-over continues.

July 8

Department of Social Relations of Massachusetts Council of Churches urges serious debate of demands for $100 million from local black churchmen group; sends letter to 1,700 member churches.

Mission society overseeing Cookman church, Philadelphia, decides group occupying building must go, court action threatened.

July 9

UCC Board for World Ministries holds open hearing on role in Interchurch Center restraining order against Forman; in concert with other parties, votes to move toward dissolving it. 200 of 700 employees of NCC ask council to reject NBEDC demands.

American Baptist unit on social concerns writes churches disavowing ideology of Manifesto but seeing demands for reparations as "gift of God's mercy"; identifies "virulent pockets of racism" in church.

July 10

Council of Episcopal Diocese of Philadelphia hears Kenyatta, demands rejected; later decision of Bishop Robert L. DeWitt and local delegates to special denominational convention in August to support NBEDC told, say resolution endorsing Manifesto programs will be introduced.

Executive Committee of United Methodist Council of Bishops repudiates ideology of Manifesto and rejects demands, cites denomination's Fund for Reconciliation; says Manifesto causes "confusion"; action reported July 15.

July 11

Interchurch Center and church agencies withdraw motion to restrain Forman, who was said to have promised no take-overs while consultations with NCC in progress.

U.S. District Judge James H. Meredith issues temporary restraining order in St. Louis barring ACTION and Black Liberation Front from church interruptions.

July 11–13

NBEDC steering committee meet in New York; word "National" dropped from title; Calvin Marshall, AME Zion pastor of Brooklyn, elected chairman; other officers chosen; plans to file for legal incorporation laid.

July 11–20

Unitarian Universalist Association's General Assembly in Boston adrift over black demands; an all-Black Affairs Council and an integrated Black and White Action vie for funding, the former wins; a $10 million reinvestment for minority economic development withdrawn by blacks after one section of program cut down to $1.6 million.

July 12

A. Dale Fiers, president of Disciples of Christ, says denomination will talk to Forman if he appears at August 15–20 General Assembly in Detroit; tells of plans which would produce $30 million for racial and urban crisis over four years.

July 13

Campbell of Riverside preaches on reparations, endorses the concept but not revolution; says "repentance without reparations is an indulgence in cheap grace."

Black P. Stone Nation (young gang) and Concerned Christians occupy unused convent in Chicago; archdiocese agrees to have parish-community discussion over building; occupiers want it for community programs.

Malcolm Boyd, Episcopal priest, issues White Manifesto supporting the black one during convention of Lutheran Church Missouri Synod; he is joined by a Catholic and a Lutheran.

Kenyatta addresses Abington United Presbyterian Church, Philadelphia, and warns of demonstrations if reparations not met; congregation includes many denominational leaders.

Black Sunday quiet in St. Louis after restraining order from St. Louis Cathedral; ACTION allowed to make presentation at St. Louis the King Church, the "Old Cathedral," other congregations visited.

July 14

Five of eight clergymen arrested as police end occupation of Cookman church, Philadelphia; group has refused to attend meeting called by Common Pleas Judge Robert Nix; church locked day before.

NCC executive committee fails to reach consensus on Manifesto response; special committee of 16 continued, another executive session set for late Summer or early Fall; NCC said to continue keeping up with federal investigation to see if any harassment involved.

July 16

Injunction against occupation of Cookman issued in Philadelphia; Judge Nix, a Negro, lashed out at "self-appointed leaders of the black movement"; no sanctions against clergy arrested recommended.

Blacks make presentation to Missouri Synod convention and are well received; ask greater assistance to black schools of denomination and overt action to combat hunger; president Jacob A. O. Preus says requests can probably be dealt with through budget.

July 17

Marshall, head of BEDC, says he is not stymied by Forman's political ideology, but rejects violence; tells how United Black Appeal will have own board; does not see white churches enthusiastically dealing with BEDC at first but coming around to it.

July 20

Rabbi Tanenbaum of American Jewish Committee says in radio broadcast that a White Manifesto of "concrete actions to transform racial justice from a pious promise to a full reality" is answer to Black Manifesto; charges BEDC had caused "shrinking back" in white community from "legitimate demands of black militant movement."

Forman presents demands to wealthy First Baptist Church, Cleveland, by prior arrangement; also appeals to local leaders to save life of Ahmed Evans, black condemned to die on charges growing out of shootings in urban disturbances.

Black Sundays visitors receive relatively warm welcome in St. Louis Catholic and Protestant churches.

July 22

Earlier decisions of two Detroit groups, one Presbyterian and one Catholic, to give $500 each to BEDC reported.

July 23

Judge Meredith extends until October 1 the restraining order against worship interruptions in St. Louis.

July 25

Letter of Disciples president A. Dale Fiers urges denominational leaders to oppose NCC recognition of BEDC; in later radio appearance he admits some "good" aspects of Manifesto in making churches see their tokenism in race relations.

July 26

Council of North Side Cooperative Ministry, an ecumenical group, reported to have promised $10,000 for black community use and a special offering for United Black Appeal.

July 27

Self-identified members of St. Louis White Citizens Council pass out leaflets at churches asking arrest and imprisonment of persons disrupting worship, call for "White Sunday" demonstrations; Black Sundays continue in peaceful manner.

July 29

Arthur Flemming, president of NCC, says blacks should be given $300 to $500 million for welfare projects by churches; estimates church assets at more than $100 billion.

August 1

Connectional Council of African Methodist Episcopal Zion Church affirms concept of reparations and asks its over one million members to participate in BEDC; retired bishop W. J. Walls is unsympathetic with Manifesto; council is nonlegislating unit composed of bishops and heads of agencies.

August 3

Judge Nix subpoenas five Philadelphia BEDC leaders to warn against church occupations, said police reported threats.

August 7

Baptist Ministers' Conference of Philadelphia supports "thrust" of Manifesto but rejects rhetoric and philosophy; later a 160-member city coalition (Reparation Action Project) of Protestants, Catholics and Jews support reparations.

August 10

New Mexico church leaders against national or local reparations, according to survey by Albuquerque *Journal* reported nationally; state United Presbyterians said upset with denomination's intimations of support for Alianza Federal de Pueblos Libre, a militant Spanish-American group, locally considered irresponsible; Alianza seeking reparations.

August 11

Ocie Pastard, Manifesto-backer from St. Louis, tells Presbyterian U.S. conference in North Carolina that "there is not enough money in our whole rich economy" to pay white debt to blacks.

August 13

BEDC given permission to keep for one year the Quaker settlement house in Chester, Pa., occupied two months earlier.

Abernathy of SCLC writes in *The Christian Century* that Forman is "a prophet to pull the covers off the economic life of the churches," but does not see himself giving much time to seeking the "limited wealth of a lethargic church"; views Manifesto as evidence of desperate need for Christian renewal.

August 15

Eight top United Presbyterian officials say in *Presbyterian Life* that Manifesto points up "intolerable inequities" but reject most of document.

Black Council in Reformed Church in America formalized as mandated by denomination's General Synod; expending $100,-000 fund for minorities turned down as sole responsibility of blacks, greater role for blacks in existing power structures asked.

August 18

Marshall, BEDC chairman, flatly denies report that Forman has been downgraded by organization.

Disciples General Assembly in Seattle rejects Manifesto by omission of channels for funding it in a four-year program designed to spend $30 million for racial and urban problems; black caucus emerges in denomination.

August 19

Census Bureau reports that 33 percent of black Americans are below poverty level as compared to 13 percent of the total population.

August 21

Central Committee of World Council of Churches turns down reparations as an attempt to distribute guilt for the past, but asks member communions to make "meaningful response"; turns down proposals of May racism consultation in the most part; wants acts of compassion going beyond financial payment; sets up secretariat to fight racism, allocated $150,000 for a budget, gives $200,000 of reserves to be distributed to "organizations of oppressed racial groups whose purposes are not inconsonant with general purposes" of WCC; wants churches to give $300,000 more.

August 29

NCC executive committee rejects Manifesto ideology but "acknowledges" BEDC as "programmatic expression of the aspirations of black churchmen"; recommends $500,000 in new money for IFCO and NCBC.

September 3

Special Convention of Episcopal Church votes $200,000 to NCBC, presumably for transfer to BEDC; first major allocation answering reparations demands.

Bibliography

Adoff, Arnold, ed., *Black on Black: Commentaries by Negro Americans.* New York: The Macmillan Co., 1968.

Baldwin, James, *The Fire Next Time.* New York: The Dial Press, 1963.

Barbour, Floyd F., ed., *The Black Power Revolt.* Boston: Porter Sargeant, 1968.

Barndt, Joseph R., *Why Black Power?* New York: Friendship Press, 1968.

Bennett, Lerone, Jr., *Black Power U.S.A.* Chicago: Johnson Publishing Co., 1967.

Borderick, Francis L., and Meier, August, eds., *Negro Protest Thought in the Twentieth Century.* Indianapolis: Bobbs-Merrill Co., 1965.

Brown, H. Rap, *Die Nigger Die!* New York: The Dial Press, 1968.

Campbell, Will D., *Race and the Renewal of the Church.* Philadelphia: The Westminster Press, 1962.

Carmichael, Stokely, and Hamilton, Charles, *Black Power: The Politics of Liberation in America.* New York: Random House, 1967.

Chambers, Bradford, ed., *Chronicles of Negro Protest.* New York: Parents' Magazine Press, 1968.

Clark, Kenneth, *Dark Ghetto: Dilemmas of Social Power.* New York: Harper & Row, 1965.

————, ed., *The Negro Protest.* Boston: Beacon Press, 1963.

————, and Parsons, Talcott, eds., *The Negro American.* Boston: Houghton Mifflin Co., 1966.

Cleage, Albert B., Jr., *The Black Messiah*. New York: Sheed and Ward, 1968.

Cleaver, Eldridge, *Soul on Ice*. New York: McGraw-Hill, 1968.

Cone, James, *Black Power and Black Theology*. New York: Seabury Press, 1969.

David, Jay, ed., *Growing Up Black*. New York: William Morrow & Co., 1968.

Davis, John P., ed., *The Negro Reference Book*. Englewood Cliffs: Prentice-Hall, 1966.

Douglass, James W., *The Nonviolent Cross: A Theology of Revolution and Peace*. New York: The Macmillan Co., 1968.

DuBois, W. E. B., ed., *The Negro Church*. Atlanta: Atlanta University Press, 1903.

Essien-Udon, E. U., *Black Nationalism*. Chicago: University of Chicago Press, 1962.

Fager, Charles, *White Reflections on Black Power*. Grand Rapids: Wm. B. Eerdmans, 1967.

Fanon, Frantz, *Black Skin, White Mask*. New York: Grove Press, 1967.

————, *The Wretched of the Earth*. New York: Grove Press, 1961.

Furnas, J. C., *Goodbye to Uncle Tom*. New York: William Sloane Associates, 1956.

Gilbert, Ben W., ed., *Ten Blocks from the White House*. New York: Frederick A. Praeger, Inc., 1968.

Goodman, Walter, *Black Bondage*. New York: Farrar, Straus & Giroux, 1968.

Gregory, Dick, *The Shadow That Scares Me*. Garden City: Doubleday & Co., 1968.

Grier, William and Cobbs, Price M., *Black Rage*. New York: Basic Books, 1968.

Hadden, Jeffrey K., *The Gathering Storm in the Churches*. Garden City: Doubleday & Co., 1969.

Hough, Joseph C., Jr., *Black Power and White Protestants*. New York: Oxford University Press, 1968.

Jones, LeRoi, ed., *Black Fire*. New York: William Morrow and Co., 1968.

————, *Home: Social Essays*. New York: William Morrow and Co., 1968.

Kelsey, George D., *Racism and the Christian Understanding of Man*. New York: Charles Scribner's Sons, 1965.

Killian, Lewis and Grigg, Charles, *Racial Crisis in America*. Englewood Cliffs: Prentice-Hall, 1964.

King, Martin Luther, Jr., *Stride Toward Freedom*. New York: Harper & Row, 1964.

_____, *Where Do We Go From Here?* New York: Harper & Row, 1967.

_____, *Why We Can't Wait*. New York: Harper & Row, 1963.

Lester, Julius, *Look Out Whitey, Black Power's Gon' Get Your Mama*. New York: The Dial Press, 1968.

Lincoln, C. Eric, *The Black Muslims in America*. Boston: Beacon Press, 1961.

_____, *Is Anybody Listening to Black America?* New York: Seabury Press, 1968.

_____, *My Face Is Black*. Boston: Beacon Press, 1964.

_____, *Sounds of the Struggle*. New York: William Morrow and Co., 1967.

Lomax, Louis, *The Negro Revolt*. New York: Harper & Row, 1962.

Malcolm X., *Autobiography*. New York: Grove Press, 1964.

Metcalf, George R., *Black Profiles*. New York: McGraw-Hill, 1968.

Muse, Benjamin, *The American Negro Revolution*. Bloomington, Ind.: Indiana University Press, 1969.

Nelson, Turman, *The Right of Revolution*. Boston: Beacon Press, 1968.

Parker, Everett C., ed., *Crisis in the Church*. Boston: Pilgrim Press, 1968.

Powledge, Fred, *Black Power—White Resistance*. Cleveland: World Publishing Co., 1967.

Proctor, Samuel D., *The Young Negro in America, 1969–1980*. New York: Association Press, 1966.

Reimers, David, *White Protestantism and the Negro*. New York: Oxford University Press, 1965.

Schuchter, Arnold, *White Power, Black Freedom*. Boston: Beacon Press, 1968.

Silberman, Charles, *Crisis in Black and White*. New York: Random House, 1964.

Sleeper, C. Freeman, *Black Power and Christian Responsibility*. Nashville: Abingdon Press, 1968.

Spike, Robert W., *The Freedom Revolution and the Churches*. New York: Association Press, 1965.

Stone, Chuck, *Black Political Power in America*. Indianapolis: Bobbs-Merrill Co., 1968.

Stringfellow, William, *My People Is the Enemy*. New York: Holt, Rinehart & Winston, 1964.

U.S. Riot Commission, *Report of the National Advisory Commission on Civil Disorders*. New York: Bantam Books, 1968.

Warren, Robert Penn, *Who Speaks for the Negro?* New York: Random House, 1964.

Washington, Joseph R., *Black Religion*. Boston: Beacon Press, 1964.

————, *The Politics of God*. Boston: Beacon Press, 1967.

Wills, Gary, *The Second Civil War*. New York: New American Library, 1968.

Wright, Nathan, Jr., *Black Power and Urban Unrest*. New York: Hawthorn Books, 1968.

————, *Let's Work Together*. New York: Hawthorn Books, 1969.

————, *Ready to Riot*. New York: Holt, Rinehart & Winston, 1968.